Should schools be colorblind?

Debating Race series

Should schools be colorblind?

LAURIE COOPER STOLL

polity

First published in 2019 by Polity Press

Polity Press
65 Bridge Street
Cambridge CB2 1UR, UK

Polity Press
101 Station Landing
Suite 300
Medford, MA 02155, USA

ISBN-13: 978-1-5095-3425-8
ISBN-13: 978-1-5095-3426-5 (pb)

A catalogue record for this book is available from the British Library.

Library of Congress Cataloging-in-Publication Data

Names: Stoll, Laurie Cooper, author.
Title: Should schools be colorblind? / Laurie Cooper Stoll.
Description: Cambridge, UK ; Medford, MA, USA : Polity Press, [2019] |
    Series: Debating race | Includes bibliographical references and index.
Identifiers: LCCN 2018061205 (print) | LCCN 2019017535 (ebook) | ISBN
    9781509534272 (Epub) | ISBN 9781509534258 | ISBN 9781509534265
    (pb)
Subjects: LCSH: Racism in education–United States. | Discrimination in
    education–United States.
Classification: LCC LC212.5 (ebook) | LCC LC212.5 .S76 2019 (print) |
    DDC 371.829/96073–dc23
LC record available at https://lccn.loc.gov/2018061205

Typeset in 11 on 15 pt Adobe Garamond
by Toppan Best-set Premedia Limited
Printed and bound in Great Britain by CPI Group (UK) Ltd, Croydon

For further information on Polity, visit our website:
politybooks.com

For my students

CONTENTS

Contents

In the aftermath of the election of Donald Trump to the presidency of the United States, schools across the country saw an uptick in the number of racist incidents occurring on campus, from the elementary level to institutions of higher learning. Ninety percent of educators who participated in a survey conducted by the Southern Poverty Law Center in 2016 immediately following the election reported their school climate had been negatively impacted, and that they did not expect racial tensions to subside anytime soon. Subsequent studies (see Barshay 2018) documenting the continued rise of racist incidents and racial bullying in educational settings following the election bear out these educators' concerns.

Yet, racism in education is nothing new; it can be traced back to the very origins of schooling in the United States. Which is why, as we continue to monitor closely these overt examples of *interpersonal racism*, we must not lose sight of the fact they are deeply connected to the *institutional racism* that remains firmly entrenched. At present, institutional racism in education is largely reinforced by policies and practices that appear "race neutral" or "colorblind" on the surface but result in very racialized outcomes for students. Today, racial disparities continue to exist in rates of graduation, educational attainment, test scores, special education referrals, and access to rigorous coursework and highly qualified teachers, to name but a few examples.

Even with the increased attention to more overt examples of racism in the US at the moment, many continue to believe the best way to deal with racism in schools is to be colorblind. But is it? This book invites a wide audience to join me in answering this question. We begin in chapter 1 by parsing the difference between colorblindness as an *ideology* and colorblindness as an *identity* and explore the empirical evidence on colorblindness and teacher bias in schools. In the second chapter, we evaluate several examples of what colorblindness looks like in schools today and discuss the consequences for teachers and students. In the final chapter, we return to the central question of the book and examine how people coming to this work from multiple entry points can engage in antiracism and social justice work in education.

I draw on several sources of knowledge in writing this book: my background in social inequalities in education; my research with school districts in the Midwestern United States; my work conducting professional development on equity-related issues with educators; and my experiences as a publicly elected school board member. It is also important to acknowledge that I come to this work not just as a sociologist who studies racism in education but as a white, straight, cisgender, female-identifying sociologist whose research in education is examined through a critical, feminist, antiracist lens. I share this because my positionality (or social location) at all times informs how I think about this work, as does my experience as a non-traditional, first-generation college student who grew up in a white, working-class family in the deep South. Because social location is central to our understandings of race and racism, readers will note that, whenever possible and where appropriate, I also include descriptors such as the race and gender identity and/or gender expression of the teachers in this book.

I have several people to thank for their help in bringing this book to fruition. First, I want to thank all the educators who graciously and generously gave of their time to provide insights. Second, I want to thank my team at Polity Press, specifically Jonathan Skerrett and Karina Jákupsdóttir, for their support throughout the production process. Third, I want to thank my research assistants, Kaitlin Meye and Tyler Besaw, for their assistance in the early stages of this book. Last but not least, I want to thank my partner, Chuck, and my children,

Emily and Anna, who have been on this journey with me every step of the way.

Finally, I wanted to dedicate this book to my students, past and present, because they continually inspire me to be a better teacher, researcher, and human. I often learn as much from them as they do from me, and I never take this for granted. I am grateful to be a part of their lives even if only for a brief time.

ONE

Race and colorblindness in schools today

I've just found that I try not to see gender, you know, race, that stuff – you just can't even look at that. They're [students] just people. I think that's the smartest way to approach it.

Mr Gira, fifth-grade teacher, Lakeview, Illinois

I've been using Mr Gira's quote with students and educators alike as the quintessential example of colorblindness (and gender-blindness) in schools since he shared his thoughts on race and education with me in the spring of 2011. At the time, Mr Gira was answering a question I posed to him about whether or not he thought race still mattered in schools. His response? The best way to deal with race (and gender) is to ignore it. Perhaps it is not surprising that a white, straight, male-identifying teacher would choose to ignore the salience of race and gender in the classroom.

But what about Ms Martin, a second-grade teacher at another school in the same district? When I asked her this question, she responded, "We need to stop thinking about this, even though it exists. We have to pretend that it doesn't exist … this *race thing*. And just move beyond that." While Ms Martin occupies a different social location than Mr Gira (indeed, she was the only black classroom teacher at Helis Elementary during my study in 2010–11), her advice on how to deal with race (and racism) in schools was the same: pretend it doesn't exist. But why? Is being colorblind the "smartest way to approach" race in schools, as Mr Gira suggests?

To answer this question, we first need to establish what it means to be "colorblind." This requires a parsing of colorblindness as an *ideology* from colorblindness as an *identity*. When it comes to the scholarship on race and racism, colorblindness has been positioned almost exclusively as an *ideology*, a system of beliefs that perpetuates the racial status quo (Bonilla-Silva 2001, 2003). According to Meghan Burke, colorblind racism is ideological because (1) it makes the reality of racial inequalities too neat and clean (e.g., some people just make bad choices, don't work hard enough, etc.); and (2) it doesn't allow us to recognize race and racism because to do so would radically change the way so many of us make sense of the world around us (2018: vii–viii). Despite what the name implies, to be colorblind doesn't literally, or even metaphorically, mean that one doesn't *see* race. As

Woody Doane points out, colorblindness is not about being "blind to color" but about the denial and downplaying of racial inequality and racist practices (2017: 976); or, as Monica McDermott puts it: "Belief in the *unimportance* of race is the sine qua non of color-blind racism" (2015: 1458; emphasis added).

When educators espouse colorblindness, it doesn't mean that they see no distinctions based on race or that they think race never matters when it comes to education. On the contrary, in an era of post-racial politics, colorblindness in schools operates in a *now-you-see-race-now-you-don't* fashion (e.g., Bonilla-Silva 2001). In other words, educators often choose when race is salient and, when expressing its salience, will use discursive strategies, including the frames of colorblind racism (Bonilla Silva 2003), to situate themselves as *not racist* (Stoll 2013).

While there has been a proliferation of research in the past three decades on colorblindness as an *ideology*, much less attention has been paid to colorblindness as an *identity* (e.g., McDermott 2015; Hartmann et al. 2017). According to Douglas Hartmann and his colleagues:

As a concept in its own right, colorblind identification differs from colorblind ideology in a number of ways. Where ideology is latent and abstract, identification is manifest and on the surface: It is asserted self-consciously and directly. At the very least, it is not hidden or "invisible" as is often the case with ideology. Ideology is directed "outward" in the sense that it makes assertions about the working of the objective social world, while identification looks "inward," and asserts only how the subjective self does or should deal with that world. Most important, it is less clear that colorblindness in this more literal and overt sense is always and necessarily in service of racism and unexamined whiteness (and may even be connected with antiracist ideals and aspirations). (2017: 867)

Given that colorblindness as an *ideology* is understood exclusively as a form of racism, can one *identify* as being colorblind and not be racist? Hartmann and his colleagues suggest the answer to this question may be "yes." Their research finds that, while most Americans, including Americans of color, identify with colorblindness directly, explicitly, and self-consciously at a personal level, this identification does not correlate directly with colorblind *ideology* (2017: 882). It appears that colorblindness as an *identity* can potentially be conceived of as aspirational and not necessarily equated with colorblind racism. At an aspirational level, espousing the idea that one "does not *see* race" might be considered by some as tantamount to saying one *should* not see race, that society *should* not be stratified along racial lines. To the extent this is the conviction of the espouser, I agree. In an ideal world, race shouldn't matter when it comes to employment, education, housing, partner selection, etc. Race *shouldn't* matter; but it does.

This is why it's important to point out, as Hartmann and his colleagues (2017) do, that colorblindness as an identity is not uniformly positive. One can aspire to be colorblind by working to dismantle racial structures that perpetuate individual and institutional inequalities, and one can aspire to be colorblind by supporting racist ideologies (i.e., colorblind racism) and practices that perpetuate the racial hierarchy. In my experience, observing and working with teachers in the Midwestern United States, when an appeal is made to colorblindness it is often positioned as aspirational; at the very least it is generally offered up as proof of an educator's enlightened attitude towards race. As one white elementary teacher in Illinois, Ms Hurley, proudly said to me one afternoon, "You know, people say to me, how many black children do you have? I don't think of them that way. I have to look at pictures with their names and think." Note the contradictions in what Ms Hurley says. In one breath, she identifies herself as colorblind – she doesn't *see* the black students in her class – but in the next breath she tells us that, in order to identify them, she has to look at their pictures, situating race as an observable physical characteristic. In other words, she acknowledges for us that, indeed, she *does* see race, but from her initial comment it is clear she doesn't believe she *should* see race. For Ms Hurley, *not seeing race*, or being colorblind, is considered admirable.

In fact, most teachers with whom I have worked assume that being colorblind is a personal virtue; that to be colorblind implies they cannot be prejudiced when it comes to race (e.g., *How can I be racist if I don't see race?*). Teachers are not anomalies. According to John Dovidio, Samuel Gaertner, and Tamar Saguy (2015: 1521), "The vast majority of White Americans perceive that the United States is currently characterized by racial and gender equality, deny any personal bias, and, in fact, assert their ability to remain color- and gender-blind in their interactions and decisions."

Further, when it comes to the teachers in my research and the ones with whom I have conducted professional development, most believe constructing colorblind classrooms serves the best interests of all their students. I define the colorblind classroom as a learning environment that is intended to serve as a microcosm of the larger society; it is a constructed space where, theoretically, opportunities are always equitable and every child is loved and valued regardless of their race or ethnicity

(Stoll 2013). When educators identify themselves as colorblind and strive to create colorblind schools, they are not typically doing so out of malevolence; in other words, they are not intentionally trying to be racist (e.g., Schofield 2009). Overwhelmingly, they do so because they see themselves as benevolent educators (López and Vázquez 2006) who believe the best way to get beyond racism in education and society at large is not, as Justice Harry Blackmun wrote in 1978, to *take account of race*, but to ignore it. But, again, is this the "smartest way to approach it?" Should schools be colorblind? This is the central question I address in this book.

Whether or not schools should be colorblind is not simply an academic question. Despite the election of Donald Trump and recent examples of very overt racism in the US (e.g., in Charlottesville, Virginia), race scholars such as Eduardo Bonilla-Silva (2018) argue that, rather than signaling a re-emergence of racism, these phenomena serve as further examples of the continued pervasiveness of colorblindness in the post-Civil Rights era. As Meghan Burke points out:

> While "traditional," overt racism has never disappeared, and may in fact be on the rise as the far right is emboldened in many places around the USA and the world, covert, colorblind racism remains prevalent. It is the

most popular way of talking and thinking about race in both major US political parties, in most schools, in our legal system, and in our conversations about race. (2018: 2)

It is in this context of heightened awareness to identity politics and the ubiquity of post-racialism that the question of whether schools should be colorblind is perhaps more salient than ever.

The ideology of colorblind racism

How to conceptualize and measure racism has often proven as controversial as how to categorize race itself. If one takes into account responses to the typical survey measures used to assess prejudicial attitudes in the US, it would appear Americans are becoming more racially tolerant. Overall, opposition to busing, residential segregation, and even interracial marriage has decreased substantially when compared with survey responses thirty or forty years ago. Qualitative studies, however, have produced data that paint a very different picture of race relations in the US. For example, while opposition to interracial marriage based on survey data has decreased precipitously over the years, when respondents are questioned using in-depth interviews as to whether they would marry someone of a different race or approve of their children marrying someone of a different race, the responses are generally negative (Bonilla-Silva 2003).

The discrepancies in data on prejudicial attitudes revealed by qualitative and mixed method studies has led to a consensus among social scientists that racism in the US has not dissipated but evolved in the post-Civil Rights era – or the "late Jim Crow era," as Kasey Henricks, a sociologist at the University of Tennessee, refers to it. If Jim Crow racism can be characterized as "blatant," the new form of racism in the US is "subtle" (Pettigrew and Meertens 1995: 58). In addition to being referred to as subtle racism, contemporary racism in the US has been termed laissez-faire racism (Bobo 1999), aversive racism (Dovidio and Gaertner 2000), symbolic racism (Sears and Henry 2003), and colorblind racism (Bonilla-Silva 2003). According to Tyrone Forman (2004), what ties these theories together is the belief that racism is rational; it is a system of oppression from which white people benefit both directly and indirectly and which they therefore have a vested interest in maintaining (e.g., Lipsitz 2006).

In 1997, Eduardo Bonilla-Silva called for a structural interpretation of racism to address what he saw as important limitations of the *idealist view* of racism that prevailed at the time. This view, he argued, confined the study of racism to the field of social psychology by reducing it to an individual-level phenomenon rooted in psychological dispositions. With its emphasis on structure, Bonilla-Silva's racialized social system theory diverges from social-psychological studies of racism that have historically focused on the *prejudice problematic* (Wetherell and Potter 1992): identifying the nature and extent of prejudice with the goal of developing interventions.

In contrast to the dominant view at the time that racism was best defined as a set of beliefs held by individuals that could potentially lead to prejudice and discrimination, Bonilla-Silva argued:

> Although "racism" has a definite ideological component, reducing racial phenomena to ideas limits the possibility of understanding how it shapes a race's life chances. Rather than viewing racism as an all-powerful ideology that explains all racial phenomena in a society, I use the term racism only to describe the racial ideology of a racialized social system. That is, racism is only part of a larger racial system. (1997: 467)

In subsequent works, Bonilla-Silva (2001, 2003) referred to the ideology of colorblind racism as the "new racism" in the post-Civil Rights era. Indeed, in his 2003 book *Racism without Racists*, whose title captured what he saw as the essence of this new racism, he stated that color-blind racism manifests in four frames used predominantly by whites to interpret information about race: abstract liberalism, naturalization, cultural racism, and minimization of racism. Of all the frames, Bonilla-Silva argues that abstract liberalism is the most important because it constitutes the foundation of the new racial ideology:

> The frame of *abstract liberalism* involves using ideas associated with political liberalism (e.g., "equal opportunity," the idea that force should not be used to achieve social policy) and economic liberalism (e.g., choice, individualism) in an *abstract* manner to explain racial matters. By framing race-related issues in the language of liberalism, whites can appear "reasonable" and even "moral," while opposing almost all practical approaches to deal with de facto racial inequality. (2006: 28; emphasis in original)

In other words, abstract liberalism allows whites to express a concern for racial inequality (and also to express pro-diversity attitudes; Stoll and Klein 2018) while simultaneously opposing race-specific policies that would directly address racial inequality. Abstract liberalism is based on the belief in individualism and meritocracy with the conviction that no group should be singled out for "special treatment" and that "individual freedoms" must be protected above all. Ironically, this allows whites to preserve the racial status quo and their own group interests by problematizing the *special* group interests of peoples of color.

The remaining frames consist of naturalization, cultural racism, and minimization of racism (Bonilla-Silva 2003). The naturalization frame explains racial phenomena in terms of natural occurrences. For instance, the choice to date only partners of the same race is rationalized not as racism but as the belief that people are *naturally* attracted to others of the same race. Cultural racism relies on culturally based arguments to explain racial inequality such as the belief that black children perform poorly in school because *black culture* does not value education. Finally, minimization of racism is based on the notion that discrimination is no longer a major determinant of life chances for racial minorities; therefore, what appear to be racialized outcomes can be explained away by factors other than racism.

My research in Illinois and Minnesota finds that teachers often rely on the frames of colorblind racism as they struggle to understand and explain race-related issues in the classroom and beyond. Yet, while it is important to hold teachers accountable anytime they perpetuate prejudice or discrimination, we must also avoid the tendency to lay the blame for institutional racism solely at the feet of teachers. Teachers' attitudes about race and racism in schooling must be connected to the institutional contexts in which they work, institutions that typically provide them with no incentive for acknowledging, let alone addressing, institutional racism (Valenzuela 1999; Chapman 2013; Cobb 2017). For example, an elementary-school teacher who works in Wisconsin recently shared with me that, when she started incorporating social justice pedagogy in her classroom in order to create a safe and inclusive learning environment for her students, she was told by her principal that she needed to "leave her politics out of the classroom." The principal even insinuated that her teaching position might be in jeopardy if she didn't. Meanwhile, this principal was oblivious to the fact that they were exercising their own politics by demanding the teacher abandon the equity work she was doing.

Indeed, education, historically as well as today, plays an important role in perpetuating dominant ideologies that are used to maintain the racial status quo. The adoption of colorblindness and post-racialism in schools is one of the ways that racial hierarchy is maintained. According to Janet Ward Schofield, colorblind policies are often adopted as a strategy to reduce race-related conflict, particularly in racially diverse schools, because administrators believe they can help protect the institution, and people in positions of responsibility in it, from charges of discrimination (2009: 282). As Marianne Modica points out, "The trend toward colorblindness in schools often masks fears of accusations of racism and stands in the way of that examination" (2015: 415). While a teacher may be an agent of the institution in which they work, they are at the same time at the mercy of the institution (Everitt 2013; Cobb 2017). Inasmuch as schools adopt the logic and politics of post-racialism, teachers are expected to do so as well.

Beyond the institutional level, there are also practical and personal reasons why educators may choose to embrace colorblindness. First, in the post-Civil Rights era, the notion of colorblindness as encapsulated in the "I Have a Dream" speech by Martin Luther King, Jr., situates colorblindness as a virtue, something many whites believe people should strive for at an interpersonal level in order to achieve racial equity, conveniently glossing over Dr King's call to dismantle structures of inequality. Further, even just *talking* about race in an era of post-racial politics has been equated by many, particularly political conservatives, with *being* racist; therefore, educators may fear that, if they discuss race with their students or engage in antiracism work, they might actually *perpetuate* racism (Modica 2015).

Second, 82 percent of public school teachers in the US are white (US Department of Education, www.ed.gov).

The racial homogeneity of the teaching force, coupled with the fact that most teachers lack the skills, training, and support needed to address racism effectively in schools, can lead to an avoidance of discussing race and racism for fear they may fail adequately and effectively to navigate conversations about both in the classroom (Priest et al. 2014; Vittrup 2016). For example, in Sara Demoiny's (2017) study of perceptions about teaching race in social studies among pre-service teachers, teacher candidates acknowledged the need to talk about race and racism in their classrooms, but they were concerned about the responses from students, parents, and administrators (see also Farago et al. 2015). According to Demoiny, "They did not want to indoctrinate their students or challenge their students' families' beliefs" (2017: 29).

Finally, in my book *Race and Gender in the Classroom* (2013), I found teachers often adopt colorblindness because they care deeply about their students and therefore want to create a world for them in which every student can succeed despite racial or ethnic identity. They wish to construct a world for their students where race and ethnicity do not matter. The reality, however, is that they still do. In the end, as Flora Farago, Kay Sanders, and Larissa Gaias point out, colorblindness remains a privilege available exclusively to whites that relieves them of the responsibility of fighting racism (2015: 43).

In addition, studies show that, when educators embrace colorblindness, there are adverse consequences for students of color. According to Marianne Modica:

> Because many white teachers believe they should be colorblind, race has become a taboo subject in many US classrooms, with serious implications for students and teachers. Silence about race denies students the skills they need to talk about race openly and honestly and the opportunity to think about how racism affects them and their relationships with others. Teachers who believe it is best to be colorblind lose the opportunity to address racial inequity in their classrooms and in their overall school programs. (2015: 397–8)

Christy Byrd found that, when students of color heard messages from teachers that ignored race, they felt less connected to others at school and had a more negative view of their academic abilities (2015: 18). Research by Meagan Call-Cummings and Sylvia Martinez (2017) suggests that, when white teachers in their study failed to acknowledge the existence of subtler forms of racism such as microaggressions, and brush them off as simply "misunderstandings," it contributed to a sense of racial battle fatigue among their Latinx students (see also Henfield 2011; Joseph et al. 2016). Anne Gregory and Edward Fergus's (2017) study found that colorblindness undermined the efficacy of social and emotional learning opportunities for marginalized students by ignoring structural biases and the positionality of educators who were charged with implementing these reforms. The research of Allison Parsons and her colleagues (2018) illustrates how authentic and meaningful relationships between parents of color and school personnel are compromised when colorblind ideologies permeate school policies and practices.

As Thandeka Chapman points out, "although the ways in which colorblind racism is enacted vary across different contexts, the outcomes are the same. It constricts the learning and development of students of color and maintains white privilege by further marginalizing students of color in academic settings" (2013: 614–15). Despite the best of intentions, not *seeing* racism harms students, especially students of color (Farago et al. 2015: 42). This is why we must "take account of race" if we want to advance racial justice (*University of California Regents* v. *Bakke* 1978).

Taking account of race and colorblindness in schools

Because one of the core assumptions of colorblind racism is that things are better now for people of color than in the past (Bonilla-Silva 2003), it is important to acknowledge the many ways in which race still matters when it comes to education. In sum, the weight of the empirical evidence demonstrates that not only are things today not necessarily better than in the past but, in some cases, such as the school-to-prison pipeline, they are worse (Kozol 2005; Alexander 2010). Yet, education is often situated as a panacea when it comes to racism and other social problems.

In the United States, education, much like race, reflects a number of interesting paradoxes. On the one hand, it is assumed to be a great equalizer and a vehicle for social mobility; on the other, education is viewed as a failing system that perpetuates inequalities and reproduces privilege (Coleman and Hoffer 1987; Blau 2003; Duncan 2005; Kozol 2005; Harry and Klingner 2006). Educational attainment is perhaps one of the best illustrations of this paradox. In general, educational attainment in the US, as in other countries with similar levels of development, is on the rise. The vast majority of Americans graduate from high school and an increasing number are graduating from college (National Center for Education Statistics 2017). Given that educational attainment is highly correlated with income, on the surface this appears to lend support to the notion that education is in fact a vehicle for social mobility.

Yet, when we disaggregate the data on educational attainment by race, we find that, while overall dropout rates have slowly declined for the past few decades, black, Hispanic, and First Nation students continue to show lower rates of educational completion, from high school to graduate school, compared to white students (National Center for Education Statistics 2017). Education in the US has never materialized as the "great equalizer" Horace Mann envisaged in 1848 (as cited in *Education and Social Inequality*; see http://faculty.trinity.edu/mkearl/strat-ed.html). Further, while exploring racism in education through the lens of statistics and national-level data is informative, I would argue it is even more important to investigate it through the everyday lived experiences of students of color.

These everyday lived experiences are directly impacted by students' interactions with teachers, administrators, and staff. This is why the research on racial bias among teachers is so troubling (Foster 1990; Rong 1996). According to George Farkas (1996), teacher bias is evident when teachers (1) perceive racial and ethnic minority students as low achievers and assign them lower test grades; and (2) assume racial and ethnic minority students have less potential and provide them with less challenging materials (see also Ferguson 2001; Wood et al. 2007; Gershenson et al. 2016; Joseph et al. 2016).

For example, historically, educators have assumed that black boys are the most *at-risk students* (Noguera 2008) and have disproportionately assigned them to special education (Delpit 2006; Harry and Klingner 2006). Academically, these educational practices can create a self-fulfilling prophecy that some scholars believe may partially explain the pervasive discrepancies in test scores between white and non-white students. According to Ronald Ferguson, "teachers' perceptions, expectations, and behaviors probably do help to sustain, and perhaps even to expand, the black–white test score gap. The magnitude of the effect is uncertain, but it may be quite substantial if effects accumulate from kindergarten through high school" (1998: 313).

In Beth Harry and Janette Klingner's study, racial bias was evident in teachers' discomfort with, even fear of, the behavioral styles of their students and in the low expectations that accompanied their discomfort (2006: 55; see also Wood et al. 2007). Further, Douglas Downey and Shana Pribesh (2004) found that white teachers' bias at least partially explained the fact that black students were consistently rated as poorer classroom citizens than white students. Similarly, Edward Morris (2005, 2007) found teachers were more likely to discipline differently the bodies of their black and Latinx students, particularly with regard to dress and manners, as opposed to their white or Asian classmates (see also Fernández 2002; Scott 2003).

More recently, Hannah Carson Baggett and Crystal Simmons's (2017) study of two white teacher candidates' awareness of racial profiling in schools found that, despite differences in teacher interpretation and personal impact, both candidates recognized that students of color were less likely to be enrolled in academically rigorous courses and more frequently and harshly punished than their white classmates (see also Chapman 2013). Further, both observed that in-service teachers were more likely to view students of color as defiant or lazy. While two is an extremely small sample size, these findings mirror those of other scholars. For example, Anne Ferguson's (2001) examination of black male students in an inner-city school found that teachers and administrators alike were inclined to identify certain students as "criminals," and Malik Henfield's (2011) analysis of black male students in a middle school in the Midwest found that students commonly experienced racial microaggressions related to their assumed deviance or criminality, racial stereotyping, and the superiority of white cultural values. Similarly, Nicole Joseph, Kara Mitchell Viesca, and Margarita Bianco (2016) found that black female students in an urban high school commonly experienced prejudice, discrimination, and low teacher expectations.

The bottom line is educators, myself included, do not live in a bubble where we are isolated from dominant narratives about race and post-racial rhetoric, and, of all the variables that affect students in schools, teachers, building administrators, and staff have the most direct impact. It is for this reason that my research in education has always focused so heavily on educators' perspectives of social inequalities. It is why I study how teachers think about concepts such as race and racism, and how their beliefs inform their pedagogy and the ways they structure their classrooms. It is why I am interested in the relationships between teachers and administrators, because teachers need support from their building and district administrators and from their local school boards if they want to challenge the racial status quo.

However, as Eduardo Bonilla-Silva and David Embrick point out, "Contrary to the popular belief that educators across the world have typically been agents for progressive racial change, the weight of the evidence suggests that most educational systems and most educators operate to maintain racial hierarchy rather than to challenge it" (2008: 334). Indeed, Dan Lortie, in his influential study of schoolteachers in 1975, found people who were attracted to the teaching profession typically favored maintaining the status quo as opposed to embracing progressive social change. Yet, despite the rich body of literature on educator bias, many of us who do work in social inequalities continue to situate teachers as important agents of change when it comes to racism in education (e.g., Noddings 1992; Allard 2004; Delpit 2006; Noguera 2008). However, the reality for the vast majority of teachers, including those who have participated in my research and those with whom I have engaged in professional development, is that this was not what they signed on for when they went into teaching.

Further, white teachers and administrators so often lack even the basic knowledge that is required to engage in racial justice work. Every semester I teach a general education course on race and ethnicity to primarily first- and second-year college students. Before the students are dismissed on the first day, I ask them to respond on a sheet of paper to two questions that will allow me some basic insights into their foundational knowledge of race: (1) What is "race"? and (2) How do you know you are the race you think you are? As a general education requirement, the course operates from the assumption that students come with no prior academic knowledge of race and ethnicity. Their answers to these two questions on day one typically reflect this. For example, the majority of students still define race at the beginning of the semester as something that is biological, genetic, or otherwise inherent and immutable. Here's the rub: I use this same exercise when I do professional development work with educators. The responses of both new and seasoned administrators, teachers, and staff reflect the responses of my first- and second-year college students (and are oftentimes more problematic).

Yet, while teachers may hold erroneous beliefs about the social, economic, and political construction of race, I have never had a teacher in my research deny that racism still exists in some form in schools today. On the contrary, many of the teachers with whom I have worked have been very forthcoming with examples of racial inequalities. Even Ms Martin, who advised that we should pretend "this *race thing*" doesn't exist, shared with me: "It just pains my heart sometimes when I walk up to the office and I see these little black boys sitting in the office. I mean, I hardly see a little white boy sitting outside the office. I don't see it." However, rather than challenging institutional racism in education, rather than taking up her concern with building administrators and colleagues, she puts the blame on the students: "I sit them down and I really get mad and say, 'Look, you are boys of color, you need to get your act together! You need to stop this!' and 'You are the ones losing out!'"

Ms Martin's actions reflect what Luigi Esposito and Victor Romano (2014) have termed "benevolent racism":

benevolent racism occurs when emphasis is placed on racial accommodation rather than transforming the prevailing racial system, all under the guise that accommodation as opposed to transformation is actually good for people of color (2014: 70; see also Esposito and Romano 2016). This is essentially the same logic Ms Martin uses when she admonishes the black male students to "get their act together" because they are the ones "losing out," as opposed to challenging the ways students are disciplined differently along racial lines or problematizing the institutional norms that marginalize students of color.

While Esposito and Romano (2014, 2016) acknowledge that benevolent racism is consistent with other forms of contemporary racism, including colorblind racism, they claim it is also different because it acknowledges and condemns white privilege. In other words, people who engage in benevolent racism are not *colorblind*: they *see* race; they *see* white privilege; they *see* racial injustice; but they continue to perpetuate racism under the pretense of benevolence. However, my own research finds that benevolent racism and colorblind racism are often interwoven. It is not atypical for teachers to acknowledge the existence of racial inequality – and, increasingly, white privilege as well. At the same time, teachers, administrators, and school board members still commonly default to colorblindness when trying to understand and make sense of these continued inequalities. When it comes to benevolent racism and colorblind racism, it is not a matter of either/or but, rather, of both/and.

In sum, despite the politics of post-racialism, I have never been hard-pressed to find teachers to agree that race still matters in the US and racism still exists in schools. But I remain hard-pressed to find teachers who know how effectively to address institutional and individual racism and have ample institutional and interpersonal support to do so. On the contrary, educational spaces today are "saturated with colorblind racism" (Chapman 2013: 614).

In the next chapter, I draw on my own research to provide some examples of what colorblind racism looks like in schools today. As we will see, in an era of post-racial politics, teachers continually vacillate between *seeing race* and *not seeing race*. Before moving on, however, I want to point out that, while we will focus our attention specifically on *race*, we cannot lose sight of the fact that systems of oppression, as Patricia Hill Collins (2000) reminds us, work together to produce injustice. In other words, to understand fully the complexities of racism in education requires us to take account of how race intersects with gender, sexuality, class, and ability status, for example. While exploring all of these intersections goes beyond the scope of this book, readers will find at times other intersections become quite obvious in the examples I provide of colorblind racism, particularly gender. Further, in my discussion of strategies for engaging in equity work in the final chapter, I will call on us to address not only *racism* in education but *all* systems of inequality and privilege.

TWO

Now you see race, now you don't

In this chapter, I provide some examples from two separate research projects I conducted in recent years of what colorblindness looks like in schools today. The first is an institutional ethnography that took place in three elementary schools in a school district in Lakeview, Illinois. In that study, I interviewed and observed eighteen teachers over the course of the 2010–11 school year, exploring their attitudes on race and gender and examining their attempts to construct equitable classrooms. The second research project was a mixed methods study in a high school in Lyons, Minnesota, during the 2013–14 school year, when I interviewed and observed ten teachers, again seeking insights into their perspectives on social inequalities and equity practices. I also administered a survey to students at Lyons High that focused heavily on their experiences with bullying and school climate (752 of the 1,043 students enrolled at the time completed the survey, representing a 72 percent response rate). To protect confidentiality, I have changed all names of people, schools, and communities where these studies were conducted.

While there are differences in methodology and scope that do not allow me to draw direct comparisons across the board, there are some important distinctions about colorblindness in education we can make from examining the findings of both studies. For example, every teacher I worked with in Lakeview and Lyons acknowledged that racism in education still exists. Yet, despite this admission, most teachers I worked with in Lakeview utilized various frames of colorblind racism (Bonilla-Silva 2003) and benevolent racism (Esposito and Romano 2014) to make claims that *we are doing all we can (and perhaps should) to address it*, while teachers in both locales tended to situate racism as a problem that existed *out there* in other districts or communities, but not where they worked. In this chapter we explore the contradictions and complexities of these ideologies. Before we do so, it's important to provide some information about Lakeview and Lyons in order to properly contextualize teachers' perspectives on race and racial inequalities in both communities.

First, Lakeview is a racially diverse, highly educated, politically liberal community of approximately 75,000 people located just north of Chicago. It is a community that prides itself on an ethos of social justice, and it's the type of place people say they move to (and stay) for the "diversity." Nevertheless, Lakeview, like most cities in the US, is very racially segregated, and this segregation is reflected in the student populations of most of its ten public elementary schools (Stoll and Klein 2018). Sixty percent of its population identifies as white, while the next two largest racial groups identify as black or African American (17 percent) and Hispanic or Latino (11 percent).

Lyons, on the other hand, is a rural community of approximately 27,500 residents, 93 percent of whom are white. In contrast to Lakeview, the closest major city is two hours away. Further, while the level of formal education in Lyons is close to the national average, at 34 percent, it is much lower than in Lakeview, where 66 percent of residents have at least a bachelor's degree. Finally, 20 percent of the population in Lyons is defined by federal guidelines as poor, as compared to 14 percent of the population in Lakeview.

In sum, both of these communities are located in the Midwestern United States, but that's where most of the demographic similarities end. Yet, the presence of colorblind racism in both places illustrates how the use of these ideologies transcends both urban and rural, both liberal and conservative, and both racially diverse and racially homogeneous communities. As we will see, colorblindness may manifest differently at times depending on the location, but its presence is observable in one way or another.

Racism in education still exists, but it's not a major problem here

Taking into account the demographic make-up of Lakeview and Lyons – and any community for that matter – is important when it comes to understanding the nuances of colorblindness. While teachers in both locales were apt to utilize the frames of colorblind racism (Bonilla-Silva 2003), and at times benevolent racism (Esposito and Romano 2014), to argue why racism in education, while still prevalent, wasn't a major problem in their communities, the reasons given for why this was the case often differed. In Lakeview, the tendency was to credit the *perceived* political and social progressiveness of the community itself. As one elementary teacher, Mr Gold, explained to me:

> You don't live in Lakeview if you are a different type of person generally. Now, all the teachers generally live in Lakeview, or they are people who have been associated with Lakeview a long time. And the ones who come

from outside soon learn the type of personality and the type of community we live in. And you'd be very out of place if your attitudes were racist and homophobic, or you had gender preferences.

Even Mr Swain, a black third-grade teacher at a predominantly black and Hispanic school in the district, told me that he didn't think racism was as "strong" in Lakeview as it was in Texas, where he had previously lived.

There were even a couple of teachers I interviewed who went so far as to say they thought the racial pendulum had swung too far in the opposite direction in Lakeview. This is encapsulated in the following conversation between myself and a white fifth-grade teacher:

LAURIE: I'm curious to know if you think racism is still a major problem in schooling today.

MS JACKSON: In some ways in Lakeview, it's become – I mean, my children have experienced *reverse racism* of being called bad names for being white, so …

LAURIE: Can you give me an example?

MS JACKSON: Of reverse racism? My sons go to Obama Magnet School and they had this big, huge African American celebration, which is fabulous …

LAURIE: For Black History Month?

MS JACKSON: Yeah … so they have this two-hour assembly every year. It's like this big fanfare. And I think that it is wonderful. But at some point I felt like here's my child, who is at a school that's pretty much 50:50. And he doesn't know the history; he has no concept of what people fought for, nothing. He's a blank slate, right? And when he looks up on stage and all he sees is a representation of like – they had two African Americans win awards at that ceremony. No white kids. So, from my perspective, I get where it comes from. But he's five, and he's looking up there going, "Oh, where am I in that picture?" Every kid should feel represented in their school. So I think that kind of balance needs to be brought back a little bit because I think we have overcome a lot.

Notwithstanding Ms Jackson's conflation of *racial prejudice* with *institutional racism*, and the fact that *reverse racism* doesn't exist, this conversation typifies the hoops that teachers often have to jump through when it comes to the politics of colorblindness. First, Ms Jackson is careful to let me know that she approves of the Black History Month celebration at Obama Magnet School. In other words, she *sees* race; she "gets it." She also acknowledges the historical struggle for racial justice.

But then she goes on to problematize the celebration for no other reason than there were no white students who received awards. She essentially evokes the minimization of racism frame by utilizing the rhetoric of *things are better now than in the past* (e.g., "we have overcome a lot ..."). Therefore, what she perceives as *special* awards for students of color at the exclusion of white students (here she uses abstract liberalism as well) needs to be "brought back into balance a little bit."

Also, note that Ms Jackson's logic for why she thinks this celebration is *reverse racism* is based on her son not understanding the lack of "representation" of white students winning awards at the Black History Month celebration. She says that he doesn't know the history of white supremacy and the struggle for black liberation in the US. Her solution? Make sure white students also get awards at the celebration as opposed to educating white students on this history and its contemporary materializations. (It's also interesting to consider why Ms Jackson, a teacher who, by her own admission, knows and understands the history of racial inequality in the US, has not taught it to her son, nor gives any indication she will do so in the future.)

Another reason some teachers claimed racism was not a major problem in Lakeview was because they and their colleagues were already doing all they could (and perhaps *should*) to construct equitable learning environments that celebrated racial diversity while at the same time mitigating racial discrimination. Of course, acknowledging racism exists and then claiming one is already adequately addressing it allows teachers to play both sides of the fence. By recognizing that racism is still a problem in schools and in society at large, teachers can situate themselves as *color-conscious* or *racially progressive*. However, dismissing the need to do more to address it, or asserting that it is has already been addressed, leaves systems of racial stratification firmly in place. My conversation with Mr Foy, a white fourth-grade teacher in Lakeview, offers a case in point.

In 2006, the Lakeview Public School District instituted the African-Centered Curriculum (ACC) program at one of its ten elementary schools where the population of black students is approximately 45 percent of the total. African-centered educational programs situate African thought, history, and culture as the foundation of all academic subjects. In Lakeview, it was created as a means to address the longstanding academic gap between white and black students in the district by offering a program built on smaller class sizes, supporting strong family–school involvement, and increasing the self-esteem and confidence of black students through an emphasis on culturally relevant curricula. From the outset, it was controversial within both the school system and the community at large.

Almost every teacher I worked with in Lakeview was opposed to the ACC program, despite the fact that none of the teachers in my study actually worked in it. In fact, with the exception of two, none of the teachers even knew anything substantive about the program. Nevertheless, across the board, teachers objected to it, including Mr Foy:

MR FOY: I'm not very supportive of it. I think it promotes segregation. I think it promotes kids are different. I'm not exactly sure what "Afro-centric" education means. How are "those kids" that much different? How is the education that much different? I think it's important to promote in our curriculum models of African American achievement and teach African American history and to celebrate cultural achievements of Africans and African Americans maybe even slightly more so than European. But, in general, we need to celebrate in the limited time we have the cultures and achievements of everybody.

LAURIE: How do you incorporate the history and achievements of African Americans into your curriculum?

MR FOY: Well, it depends. We see it mostly in social studies. When we study a particular topic. I think the social studies curriculum is pretty good about including

African and Hispanic elements of the culture, Native American elements. We're going to start a unit on Illinois history pretty soon and there's a focus on both the experiences of Native American history and the experience of African American history and Illinois history. Many of the books that we read that are part of the curriculum are by African American authors and about the African American experience. I just finished reading aloud to my class "The Watsons go to Birmingham in '63." We talk a lot about that. We talk a lot about the Civil Rights movement. So it's there. Does it need to be more? I suppose … I'm sure I could do more. But I'm fairly confident that I include as much as I should.

In this exchange, Mr Foy evokes both benevolent racism (Esposito and Romano 2014) and colorblind racism (Bonilla-Silva 2003) to dismiss the validity of the ACC program. He implies that black students are harmed by what he sees as the segregationist nature of the ACC program (benevolent racism), but his comment about needing to celebrate all cultures utilizes abstract liberalism to imply that black students are essentially getting *special treatment* because the program focuses on an Afro-centric curriculum (this is similar to Ms Jackson's comments above about *special awards* for black students). His objection is akin to "all cultures matter." Mr Foy also evokes colorblindness when he says he thinks the ACC program promotes the belief that kids are "different," which he clearly opposes, and then asks rhetorically how "those (black) kids" are "that different." Further, Mr Foy tells me that he knows for sure he *could* do more to incorporate the experiences of people of color into his curriculum, but he is fairly confident he includes as much as he *should*. This opinion, of course, is based solely on his social location as a white, straight, male-identifying teacher.

Mr Gira, the white fifth-grade teacher to whom we were introduced in chapter 1, and who suggested being colorblind was the smartest way to approach race, taught in the same school as Mr Foy. He also objected to the ACC program because he thought it was unnecessary in the school district today:

> I know very little about ACC. I remember when it was initiated. I think it's more important that kids just … it's nice to provide them with interesting material, but I think we're really aware of that now. I think we provide a mix of all types of literature. We go out of our way to make sure that we cover the holidays and the special events and the people that are important to our history. That's not a problem in this district. And if "those kids" get the right training up front, it won't be an issue. Now, if you have kids that are already

behind and you're trying to get them more interested in school that might help them. It might, but I don't have any statistics to prove that that's been – they've been doing ACC now for several years, so I don't know if they can point to anything that says this has been successful and here's why.

Despite acknowledging that he knows very little about the ACC program, Mr Gira states that he doesn't think it's necessary because teachers in the general education curriculum are already providing culturally relevant material and engaging in multiculturalism. In fact, he tells me that teachers in Lakeview "go out of their way" to do so and that a lack of culturally relevant material or multiculturalism is "not a problem in this district." Mr Gira's assertions, like Mr Foy's, are based solely on his own positionality, not on the perceptions of his students of color. The lack of empirical evidence to support his argument is ironic given that Mr Gira alludes to the lack of such evidence to demonstrate the success of the ACC program, which, although he is unaware of it, he admits may exist.

It's also important to note that Mr Gira refers to culturally relevant materials not as critical, empowering, or necessary for students of color, but as "interesting." In addition, he states that, if "those (black) kids" get the "right training up front," he doesn't think there would be a need for a program such as ACC unless there are students who are "already behind" and not interested in school. Mr Gira's use of the term "training" as opposed to "learning" suggests he is referring not to black students' early childhood school experiences but to early socialization in the home. This assertion is an example of cultural racism: here *black culture* is implicated in students' potential academic struggles and lack of interest in schooling (Bonilla-Silva 2003). Some scholars also refer to this as a cultural deficit model (e.g., DePouw 2012).

Mr Foy and Mr Gira were not the only male teachers in my study who thought they, their colleagues, their schools, and/or their district were already doing enough to address racism adequately in education. Mr Gold, a male teacher of Middle Eastern descent, who taught in the same school, remarked to me concerning racial inequality, "We try very hard at this school to give every child an education, make every child feel comfortable here. All the teachers in this school do. I can't think of a single one that doesn't." Like Mr Foy and Mr Gira, Mr Gold could offer no empirical evidence for his claim that all teachers in his school worked "very hard" to create an inclusive, safe, and welcoming learning environment for students of color in the building. Even Ms Smith, a white bilingual education teacher with master's degrees in black studies and English as a second language, who taught at the only school in the district that offered the ACC program and spoke passionately about the importance of equity work in education, told me, "This particular district, I feel that they really do encourage an equal playing field for everybody within the classroom ... Everything is possible in this district."

In the end, working in a school district in a racially diverse, politically liberal community with a stated commitment to multiculturalism and self-professed equity-minded teachers was all the "evidence" some teachers needed to claim racism was not a major problem in Lakeview. Teachers in Lyons, on the other hand, couldn't point to the racial diversity or social progressiveness of their district or community to make the argument that racism was more of a problem in other places, but they could assert that things were better now than in the past. Ms Hamilton, a white social studies teacher, offers a case in point:

It's better than it used to be, because when I first came here ... this was a white community and so it's much more diverse now. Especially when the Hmong people moved in. There was a big community uproar about all these Hmong people coming in. But that was after the Vietnam War, and these Hmong people were saviors of America's soldiers! They came in and I thought they were heroes. A lot of people didn't in the community. The black community is coming primarily from Chicago, and they're coming from, lots of times, very violent experiences. If I ask, "Have any of you known anyone who's been shot?," it's pretty prevalent in that group.

What is particularly perplexing about Ms Hamilton's comments is that Lyons is *still* very much a white community with very little racial diversity. She also evokes the minimization of racism frame by claiming that the situation in Lyons is *better than it used to be*. However, right after advancing this colorblind assertion, she centers the racial identity of Hmong community members to situate herself as a benevolent white person who recognizes them as "heroes" – unlike other (racist) whites who caused a "big uproar" when the Hmong arrived. Ms Hamilton also centers the racial identity of the black community in Lyons when she makes the sweeping generalization about their supposed migration from *violent* neighborhoods in Chicago. Her use of colorblind racism followed by her race-specific comments about Hmong and black community members is a classic example of how colorblindness manifests in a *now-you-see-race-now-you-don't* fashion in an era of post-racialism.

Ms Hamilton wasn't the only teacher in Lyons to use the minimization of racism frame. As Ms Miller, a white Spanish teacher at Lyons High, told me:

> I think that we have spent more time dealing with racial inequities and not with inequities of income. I think in our country, there's still that … if you just pull yourself up by your bootstraps, there's work opportunities. It's because of your laziness that you're not making the money you should be making. And I think that that's probably one of our biggest problems. I realize we have racial issues and things like that, but I think that's one we're not addressing.

While Ms Miller acknowledges that "racial issues" are still a problem, she essentially situates socioeconomic inequality and racial inequality as mutually exclusive when she claims educators have "spent more time dealing with racial inequities" and there is not enough attention being paid to social stratification. This was in fact the most common usage of the minimization of racism frame I found in both studies: the notion that the tables had turned and social class was now a greater determinant of life chances than race (Wilson 1978). Yet, this logic clearly ignores not only the fact that, in general, people of color in the US are overrepresented among the poor (US Census Bureau, www.census.gov) but also that students coming from lower socioeconomic backgrounds in Lakeview and Lyons are overwhelmingly students of color. Here, social class and poverty are essentially treated as if they are race-neutral.

Finally, while several teachers in Lakeview referenced the racial diversity of their community, along with a perceived love for and appreciation of that diversity, as evidence that racism wasn't a major problem, when teachers in Lyons tried to make the same argument, interestingly, they based their assertion on how *few*, as opposed to how *many*, students of color they had (such students account for only 12 percent of the student body at Lyons High). As Ms Dempster, a white English teacher, said to me, "I think that the racism piece, the significance of it as a problem, depends on the make-up of it at the school." There are two major problems with Ms Dempster's logic. First, it assumes "race" applies only to people of color – in other words, white people have no race; therefore, schools with mostly white students can't have a problem with racism (e.g., Lewis 2004, 2005). Second, this logic (e.g., "We don't really have a problem with race in our [mostly white] school!") provides the justification to reframe racially charged incidents when they occur at school in race-neutral ways. This was nowhere more evident at Lyons High than when it came to bullying.

When racism becomes bullying

When I began my study at Lyons High, it was not my intent to study "bullying" until I attended a school-wide assembly in September 2013. The purpose of the assembly was not to educate students on bullying but to celebrate difference and encourage them to practice tolerance by reaching out to others who were outside their social circles. The gymnasium was filled to capacity that morning with freshmen, sophomores, juniors, and seniors congregated in assigned quadrants in the bleachers. Dr Turner, a professional education consultant from California, served as the facilitator. He was one of very few African Americans in attendance (it is important to note that not only is Lyons High a mostly white school in terms of the student body, but there were no teachers or staff of color who worked in the building at the time of my study).

Dr Turner's "diversity pep talk" concluded with an exercise in which he asked students to stand silently if he read a statement aloud that resonated with them. Among the statements he read were two that directly related to bullying: (1) *I have experienced or know someone who has experienced bullying*; and (2) *I know someone who has attempted or committed suicide as the result of bullying*. Almost every student in the gym stood when

Dr Turner read each of these statements. While visually powerful, this exercise, of course, revealed nothing about incidence or prevalence when it came to bullying and suicide at Lyons High. Indeed, one recent study found that some students grossly overestimate the prevalence of bullying and the perceived support for it among their peers (Perkins et al. 2011: 716). Still, I made the decision then to include questions about bullying when I interviewed teachers and to be attuned to any episodes of bullying types of behavior related to race in my field observations.

I quickly found that, even when my discussions with teachers turned to bullying, the examples they provided of bullying they witnessed or that students reported to them almost always involved racism (as well as sexism and homophobia). For example, in my conversation with Ms Dempster, she connected bullying at Lyons High with racist slurs. When I asked if she could provide an example, she replied: "I hear, 'O look at you – such a *nigger*!' a lot. That happened in my room actually. I had to kick a white boy out. I said 'I'm sorry, you don't use that word in here.' And he was out. But it's often in the halls, you know." Note in this exchange that at the same time Ms Dempster clearly articulates her disapproval of this behavior in her classroom, and lets me know she took swift action to make sure it didn't continue, she acknowledges that race-related bullying often takes place in the halls. In other words, these are behaviors that largely happen outside of her purview. Ms Dempster's attitude, like those of some of the teachers in Lakeview referenced above, is one of *I'm doing all I can.*

Other teachers in Lyons also mentioned race specifically when asked about examples of bullying, as the following exchange with Ms Hayes, a white special education teacher, illustrates:

MS HAYES: Mostly, I have seen a little bit of bullying with race. Just here and there. 'Cause a few years ago I had some white kids that picked on a black kid in a class.

LAURIE: When you say "picked on," what do you mean?

MS HAYES: They made comments. Racist comments to a kid.

Similarly, Ms Miller shared with me some of the racist comments she heard students make: "I notice the Latino ones more just because of what I teach. The assumption that their parents are illegal; the assumption that they don't speak English as their first language; the assumption that they call people who speak Spanish, 'Spanish': 'They're Spanish!' No, they're not!"

In all of these examples, we see blatant instances of racism being subsumed under a race-neutral term:

"bullying." What is interesting about this practice is that, on the one hand, teachers' condemnation of these incidents suggests a heightened awareness of race and racism on their part (as opposed to colorblindness). But the fact that these teachers framed such instances exclusively as *bullying* as opposed to clear-cut examples of *racism* erases the centrality of race and the racial bigotry that underlies these comments. Indeed, bullying in schools is typically understood by educators as race-neutral (at least on the surface), since anti-bullying policies rarely reference the social location or positionality of students.

For example, Lyons School District has had a state-mandated bullying policy in place since 2005. According to this policy, any behavior that can *objectively* be labeled as intimidating, threatening, abusive, or harming can be considered "bullying" *if* it is determined by school administrators that a power imbalance exists between the perpetrator(s) and victim(s) *and* the behavior constitutes a pattern or interferes with a student's educational opportunities, performance, participation in school functions, or ability to receive school benefits, etc. This policy makes no reference to race/ethnicity (or gender identity/expression, sexuality, etc.) and is essentially what race scholars would call "race-neutral." Yet again, when teachers spoke of bullying, they almost always linked it with racism (as well as sexism and homophobia). Clearly, bullying was not race-neutral, and therefore calling these incidents bullying as opposed to racism only reinforces colorblindness.

Further, Ms Dempster was not the only teacher in Lyons to suggest she was doing all she could; this was actually a common sentiment I found among teachers when it came to bullying, including racially motivated bullying. As Mr Baines, a white woodworking teacher, said to me, "We keep a close eye on it. I go over right away if I suspect bullying and we talk it out and see what's going on." Similarly, Ms Hamilton, the teacher who claimed Lyons *used to be* a white community, told me, "I have a whole thing on bullying that I do. I have pretty clear expectations, and if I hear something, I talk about it. If you've got a swastika on your arm, this is offensive to people."

While in my Lakeview study I had no statistical data from students to corroborate teachers' claims they were doing all they could to create inclusive, safe, and welcoming learning environments, this was not the case in Lyons. Despite teachers' assertions there that they did not tolerate bullying and that they swiftly and effectively addressed it when they witnessed or suspected a student was being bullied, data from the student climate survey I developed painted a different picture. Of the students at Lyons High who took the climate survey (72 percent of the student body), 66 percent indicated the adults in their school rarely or never noticed bullying; 55 percent that they rarely or never tried to stop bullying; 49 percent that they rarely or never talked openly about bullying; 43 percent that they rarely or never supported students who were bullied; 53 percent that they rarely or never disciplined those who bullied; and 50 percent that they rarely or never listened to both sides of the story. In addition, 41 percent of students who took the survey indicated the adults in their school ignored bullying sometimes, often, or all the time; 23 percent that they made excuses for bullies sometimes, often, or all the time; and 23 percent that they disciplined those who were bullied sometimes, often, or all the time. Clearly, there was a disconnect between teachers' and students' perceptions of bullying at Lyons High.

Beyond these descriptive statistics, I also found when it came to teachers' perceptions of bullying that there was a lack of racial symmetry in both *perceptions of victimization* and the *enforcement of discipline* that reflected the unacknowledged intersections of white privilege and racial oppression – in other words, colorblindness. For example, teachers' accounts of bullying suggested that they, as well as administrators, handled situations differently when students of color were *being bullied* as opposed to when they thought students of color were *doing the bullying*. Again, this illustrates the ways teachers vacillate between *seeing race* and making appeals to *colorblindness* depending on the racial or ethnic identity of the students in question. Ms Coxey, a white special education teacher, shared her own frustrations with this "double standard":

I know that my peers are unaware of the extent of bullying at Lyons High, because they don't want to be aware of it. Are they aware of the five graffiti showing a lynching of a black person and "Kill all Niggers" that were around the school? No, they were erased as quick as they could be. Five or six years ago, there was a single sign that said, "Kill All Whites! Whites Will Die May –" whatever. And we got cops lining up with guns! We got a third of our student body not showing up, and it's in the newspaper. We have *five* pictures of lynching. And the school administrators and teachers are discussing – and they don't know that I know this because I had a friend that was in the counseling circle – about they think that black students are doing it to get attention because only black students noticed the graffiti that said, "Kill All Niggers." White people passed by it like they passed the swastikas any given day written in the boys' bathroom. It's people of color who notice hate messages, and I am sorry that it looks like maybe people of color are looking for attention, but they are not. Hate speech is here.

In this example, Ms Coxey points out the extreme measures teachers and administrators took to ensure that white students were protected from *perceived* violence by students of color. However, according to Ms Coxey, this outrage and subsequent action were not extended towards students of color with regards to the lynching graffiti.

There were also examples provided to me of teachers and administrators disciplining differently the bodies of their students of color (e.g., Morris 2005, 2007) as compared with their white students. In the following, Ms Harnish, a white English as a Second Language (ESL) teacher, shares a story about how the clothing choices of some Asian American students were construed as gang-related by the administration at Lyons High:

A couple years ago now there was an incident with some of my boys. I don't even remember how it all started to be honest, but they all ended up wearing red. Asian boys, red on the same day. I don't even remember who it was that called them down to the office and said, "Is this gang-related?" These boys would *never* – I can tell you in a million years – be part of a gang. In fact, their families would kill them. Literally kill them probably before they would ever get involved in a gang. The dads would be on them. It wasn't affiliated with a gang. And so that made the boys even more angry, and I ended up saying to the administration, "To kind of accuse them of being a part of a gang because they're all wearing red is ridiculous. Where is this coming from?" I had to do a lot of de-escalating of that whole incident, too, with the kids because it just made them more angry that they were called down to the office. And, like I said, I can't even remember how it started, but it just kept building and building and building.

Although there was no evidence to suggest these students had ever been associated with violence, they were defined as a threat to student safety and placed under suspicion by teachers and administrators because they were wearing the color red and all happened to be of Asian descent. According to Ms Harnish and Ms Coxey, this degree of hyper-vigilance was not applied to situations when white students, as opposed to students of color, were identified as the aggressors.

In sum, when it comes to bullying and race, I believe subsuming acts of racism (as well as sexism and homophobia) under the umbrella term "bullying" allows educators to focus their attention on remediating individual acts of bigotry while institutional racism remains firmly in place. For example, at Lyons High it was not uncommon for teachers to reprimand students for their *word choices* when it came to bullying-types of behavior (e.g., "You can't say the 'N-word' in my class!") but not to engage in conversations about how these word choices reflect and perpetuate systems of racial oppression. When racism occurs, but we decide to call it something race-neutral, we are exempting ourselves from the responsibility of directly addressing racial inequalities; we are perpetuating colorblind racism.

The white backlash

Every administrator and teacher I have ever worked with has expressed to me a commitment to equity in education (e.g., "Of course, our schools should be equitable for all students!"). When educators claim they care about and are committed to constructing equitable learning environments, I do not believe the majority of them are being disingenuous. At the same time, I am fully aware that "equity" in education circles has become a buzzword, much like "multiculturalism" or "trauma-informed." In this political and cultural context, I realize I would be hard-pressed to find a teacher or administrator who would tell me they were *opposed* to equity, just as I have yet to come across a teacher who will deny that racism is still a problem in schooling (this is precisely why, when I study inequalities in education, I interview teachers *and* do multiple observations with them so I can record any instances in which philosophy and pedagogy do not match).

Yet, despite the examples of colorblind racism (Bonilla-Silva 2003) and benevolent racism (Esposito and Romano 2014) I have shared in this chapter, I would be remiss if I did not acknowledge there are a few of teachers with whom I worked in both Lakeview and Lyons who I would say were genuinely equity-minded and not afraid to speak out when they saw injustice. In fact, Ms Coxey, the white special education teacher at Lyons referenced above, is one of the most social justice-oriented teachers I have ever met. It was Ms Coxey, in fact, that allowed for my initial entrée into Lyons High School. At the time, she was a member of the Lyons School District diversity committee. The committee, with approval from the district, decided to hold a day-long mandatory staff development meeting on white privilege before the start of the 2012–13 school year. Because of my expertise in this area, Ms Coxey reached out to me to see if I would help facilitate some of the discussions that day.

Granted, there was some grumbling about this training among some of the teachers in the district, and a few complained to the district office. Regardless, their attendance was mandatory. At the time, I remember finding it hard to fathom that such training was taking place in a community such as Lyons when I had only recently finished the study in Lakeview, where even the few social justice-oriented teachers didn't feel they would have the necessary support to talk about systems of privilege and oppression, such as white supremacy, in a school district that prided itself on being multicultural. Why was dismantling white privilege on the agenda in the Lyons Public School District but not in Lakeview? I believe the answer to this question in large part is because of Ms Coxey and teachers like her.

By the time I met Ms Coxey, she had definitely developed a reputation at Lyons High. As she described to me, she often felt as if a target was on her back because she was so vocal about racism at the school. At the time, she was also the faculty advisor for the sole social justice-oriented student organization at Lyons High, UNITY. "Sometimes when I walk down the hall," she told me, "I feel like people are thinking, 'Uh, oh, here she comes again!'"

When I spent time with Ms Coxey, she would often share stories of the obstacles she encountered in her efforts to advance equity at Lyons High. The following exchange between the two of us illustrates some of these struggles. She begins by describing what happened when, as the faculty advisor for UNITY, she tried to get approval to hold a day of silence at the school to recognize violence against the LGBTQ community.

MS COXEY: And the site team – it's a group of teachers and administrators – they decide what's gonna go on in the school and then you write up a little proposal, and if it interrupts the school day, then they're supposed to have a say about it. And I've never gone through them before, but recently I've thought, "OK, I'll do what everybody's expected to do." So, the site team came to see me last year, the head of it, and she just wanted me to know that they had approved our day of silence, except that they had concerns about the nature of my announcements. They just wanted to make sure that they were "appropriate." I said, "Excuse me, explain to me what you think 'appropriate' means. They're very appropriate."

LAURIE: Can you give me an example of one?

MS COXEY: She's like, "Well, apparently you said something about police last time." And it took me five minutes. I'm standing there, and she's copying. I said, "Oh. My. God. I know which one you're talking about. When I announced you should know your rights when you're stopped by police officers. Is that the one that was offensive to you?"

And that was the one that was offensive. Yes. Apparently, they felt that I was dissing authority. [laughs] Oh, my God! What is offensive! What is offensive to people! Oh, how about the time when Jackie [white principal at Lyons High] ripped me a new one [reprimanded her quite harshly], like three years ago, because UNITY had done a Christopher Columbus Day poster that said "The Beginning of the End," and we used all historical quotes in terms of the number of Native Americans who were murdered and that it was genocide. And we wrote something, but it was a primary source that we'd used. And she's, like, "Alyssa, the staff is just not ready for it." I said, "It's a 500-year-old truth, Jackie." She's, like, "Imagine what I felt coming in here on a Saturday and seeing that poster." [laughs] It's like they don't understand. And that's when I get blown away: when I don't understand what they don't understand.

Ms Coxey had also been banned from making announcements about white privilege over the PA system:

LAURIE: Whose decision was it to cancel some of your announcements?

MS COXEY: That was a principal decision.

LAURIE: You were banned from talking about white privilege?

MS COXEY: On the announcements. And, in fact, nobody told me that they were cutting my announcements on white privilege and then I found they had been intentionally cut. Nobody has announcements taken! I was censored. They were completely taken off, and Jackie's, like, "People are not ready to hear this." So, then when UNITY members came around I told the kids, "The only persons who can do these announcements are you, 'cause they're gonna have to say no to you, and they won't."

Ms Coxey also raised concerns about the lack of racial diversity in certain student organizations at Lyons High. Here she patently illustrates her colleagues' use of abstract liberalism to dismiss these concerns: "I've talked about National Honor Society being 99.9 percent white. Student Council being white. And then the teachers say, 'Well, that's black students or non-white student's *choices*. Why don't they step up? Why don't they become leaders?' They just don't get it."

Finally, Ms Coxey also objected when the only person of color at Lyons, a school counselor, was let go, apparently stemming in part from her thick accent: "I talked to Jackie personally about it. She's, like, 'Alyssa, the students can't understand her.' I was, like, 'Fuckin' A!' [laughs] Focus! You know? I mean, if we only provide a Minnesota accent to kids, how will they ever learn how to – it doesn't take that much effort to just think a little bit, and say, 'I'm sorry, I did not understand what you said.' "

Then, there was also Ms Roberts, a white first-grade teacher in Lakeview, who challenged the parent–teacher organization and her colleagues over a very problematic school fundraiser:

> You have to pay forty bucks to go to it. It's an event for only parents, only adults. Which, right away, a lot of people don't leave their kids at home for things like that. And they have a silent auction and there are teachers that you can bid on to spend special time outside of school with. So I've brought it up several times at staff meetings because I feel like there's nothing more biased than that event. It just really, really bothers me. I do have my little circle of support and some people don't participate in the silent auction. But it hasn't been stopped and the PTA felt very attacked, felt like I was not appreciative of all their work and stuff. I was called a "socialist."

Ms Roberts and Ms Coxey are both great examples of teachers who stood up to racial inequalities in their schools. But as both point out, there has been a price to pay for doing so. As Ms Coxey recently wrote to me:

> When we visit with teachers (and others) about real equity work, we need to prepare them. This is brutal work, and it will be met with retribution. Others in education have experienced this as well. Some have also been broken by what they discovered (the intentionality of racism/disparities). Others are afraid to speak up for fear of losing their jobs. Those of us who tried to engage in conversations about equity were met by full-scale white backlash. Whites and those who are assimilated into whiteness don't want to hear any other narratives that make them feel "bad" about themselves. They want the "other" to change. Personally, I continue to believe that, until organizations are willing to put aside their egos and to form coalitions based on common goals, nothing will change. In order to dismantle a system that is intentionally designed to create inequity, we need serious coalition building between like-minded organizations for legal change. Individually, we will fail.

At the time Ms Coxey wrote to me, she was on medical leave resulting from job-related stress and trauma. When another faculty member at Lyons stepped in and volunteered to advise UNITY, they were told by the new principal there was no need for a group like UNITY any longer at the high school.

As the examples of Ms Coxey and Ms Roberts illustrate, when teachers speak out about racism (or other social inequalities) in their schools, they often face a "white backlash," as Ms Coxey put it. The fear of this retribution, coupled with the pervasiveness of post-racial rhetoric in schools, provides more incentive for educators to embrace and promote colorblindness than it does for them to challenge it. Yet, colorblindness harms students, especially students of color (Byrd 2015; Modica 2015; Gregory and Fergus 2017).

As Lisa Delpit argues, "If one does not see color, then one does not really see children" (2006: 177). What are the consequences of teaching students of color that race no longer matters when their lived experiences so often demonstrate otherwise? First, this promotes a false narrative of meritocracy by furthering the notion that, if students of color and their families experience hardship or inequalities of any kind, it must be due to their own personal failings, not institutional or interpersonal racism. As Meghan Burke points out, "Colorblind racism asserts that there are no real problems with racism in our society, that challenges stem from individuals rather than our institutions and collective thinking and behavior" (2018: 1). Further, colorblindness on the part of teachers prevents students both from learning how to talk about race and from having to be self-reflexive about how racism affects them and their relationships with others (Modica 2015: 397–8). In sum, colorblindness stands in the way of our being able to address racism and white supremacy in schools.

Conclusion

This chapter highlights two overarching issues when it comes to addressing racial inequalities in schools today. First, as we saw from interview data in both Lakeview and Lyons, despite acknowledging that racism is still a problem and expressing a commitment to equity, teachers tend to default to the frames of colorblind racism (Bonilla-Silva 2003) and, at times, benevolent racism (Esposito and Romano 2014) in ways that perpetuate the racial status quo. Indeed, even when teachers speak of *antiracism* work, they often situate it as a colorblind endeavor, as illustrated by the following exchange between myself and Ms Hurley, the third-grade teacher who told me she had to look at pictures of her students to tell if they were black:

LAURIE: How would you define an "antiracist" teacher? What does that to mean to you?

MS HURLEY: Antiracist … well, somebody who makes it an issue in your classroom. I think you live it; I don't think you just talk it. I think you keep it in your mind. And it's kind of, like, I go to the cafeteria or outside and all the black children are playing together and the white children. I'm present to that. I'm conscious of it and then the years when that has been so, I mix the kids up and I assign them groups so they can experience one another without telling them. I think that's antiracist so they learn they can work with anybody. Because that's one of the beauties of having a school that is diverse.

LAURIE: So would you consider yourself an antiracist teacher?

MS HURLEY: Probably. Yeah. I don't think you have to speak it. I think you have to live it. And you have to find ways to almost be *subversive* and conscious about it, like teaching the kids about Supreme Court and about Roe, about segregation and integration and that whole thing. That's not in the curriculum but I do it every year, and those words have become part of their language. And I keep them up front and center because they are so important. So I guess I would be an antiracist teacher. [laughs]

In my conversation with Ms Hurley, she offers some examples of the practice she uses to advance racial equity: (1) she assigns racially heterogeneous groups in her classroom and (2) she teaches her students about segregation and integration although it is not part of the curriculum. However, she also tells me that this work – work she is labeling as "antiracism" – should be "subversive." Indeed, when I ask her if she thinks of herself as an "antiracist" teacher, she says, "I don't think you have to speak it." She also talks about antiracism as something you "keep in your mind." It is clear that Ms Hurley believes antiracism is something one need not verbalize explicitly but should instead model. I completely agree that antiracism must be modeled, but, when we engage in the kinds of practices Ms Hurley identifies without also talking about why we are doing this work, why it is important, and why it is still necessary, we are essentially decentering race yet again and perpetuating colorblindness. It is also important to note that all of the examples of antiracism Ms Hurley references are interpersonal. There is no mention of structural-level antiracism work that involves changes to policies or laws.

The other issue this chapter highlights is that, when it comes to teachers who are genuinely engaging in antiracism work, they are often met with condemnation and receive little or no support from their administrators and/or colleagues. I have even worked with teachers whose principals have issued not-so-veiled threats that their contract would be terminated if they continued their "social justice agenda." The costs for educators are not just career-related: the stress of fighting what equity-minded teachers often describe as an "uphill battle" can also take a physical and mental toll, as evidenced by Ms Coxey, who after years of advocating for students and families of color that were experiencing blatant racial discrimination was diagnosed with symptoms of PTSD.

Given the numerous examples I provide of colorblind-ness in this chapter, it is obvious there is much work that remains to be done to address racism in our schools. It is also obvious, given the empirical evidence, that being colorblind is *not* the "smartest way" to approach race and racism in education, as Mr Gira suggested. So what can be done? In the final chapter, I return to the central question of this book and outline some strategies for doing antiracism in education for people coming to this work from multiple entry points.

THREE

Doing antiracism in schools

Should schools be colorblind? If we are considering this question from a strictly theoretical perspective, then perhaps we might be inclined to answer "yes": yes, schools should be colorblind to the extent that race *should not* matter and society *should not* be stratified along racial lines. Yet, race continues to matter in schooling precisely because society *is* stratified along racial lines, and the way to deconstruct racial stratification is not by denying the significance of race but by changing policies, practices, and laws to ensure racial equity. Put simply, colorblindness harms students, especially students of color (Chapman 2013; Byrd 2015; Farago et al. 2015; Call-Cummings and Martinez 2017; Gregory and Fergus 2017). Therefore, from a practical, evidence-based standpoint, the answer to the question of whether schools should be colorblind is a resounding "no."

How do we move from being *colorblind* to being *color-conscious*, especially those of us coming to this work from multiple entry points? One place I think is helpful to begin is with an understanding of the concept of *everyday antiracism* (Pollock 2008). According to Pollock, "everyday antiracism requires both addressing people's experiences in the world as racial group members and refusing to distort people's experiences, thoughts, or abilities by seeing them only or falsely through a racial lens" (2008: xix). The guiding question for educators, according to Pollock, is "when does treating people as racial group members help them and when does it harm them?" (ibid.: xviii). Knowing when to call attention to race in order to *address* an injustice and when not to call attention to race because doing so would *create* or *perpetuate* an injustice requires a level of skill and nuance that must be developed through relationship-building with students of color and their families, personal and professional development, and a lot of critical self-reflection. Even then, there will be times when we get it "wrong." When that happens, we should welcome the opportunity to learn from our mistakes, make amends if possible, and then continue the work.

In this final chapter, I offer some suggestions for how teachers, administrators, school boards, and community members can engage in everyday antiracism (Pollock 2008). Of course, there are many other constituent groups that also bear responsibility for ensuring that all students have access to welcoming, inclusive, and safe learning environments. While this chapter doesn't address all stakeholders specifically, it is my hope that the suggestions offered here will spark critical discussions across the board about how we can work to dismantle white supremacy and racism in schooling. Further, while these suggestions are offered to challenge the racial status quo specifically, in what follows I also use more expansive terms such as "equity" and "social justice" because, as intersectionality scholars remind us, systems of oppression such as racism, sexism, ableism, classism, transphobia, and homophobia work together to produce injustice (Collins 2000).

Before we begin, there are three fundamental non-negotiables we must understand when it comes to doing equity work in education. To illustrate the first, I'd like to share a brief vignette. One of the courses I regularly teach at the University of Wisconsin-La Crosse is "Schools and Society." Most of the students who sign up for this course are sociology majors, but, given its nature, I always have a few education majors as well. A couple of years ago, I had a white, male-identifying education major named Colin enroll in my class. At the time, he was preparing to do his student teaching the following semester. I had the pleasure of getting to know him fairly well, and I learned that he was very passionate about social justice issues in education, too. One afternoon towards the end of the semester, he raised his hand in class and asked me, with equal parts desperation and exasperation, "How do you decide what to focus on when you are doing equity work in schools? There are so many issues I care about! As teachers, we have so many responsibilities, so many things on our plates. We can't do it all, so how do we choose what to include?"

While I completely understand where Colin's question was coming from, to be clear, this is the *wrong* question when it comes to equity work. The bottom line is this: regardless of whether we come to this work as teachers, administrators, or community members, or from any other entry point, we must begin with the fundamental understanding of equity that is reflected in the first non-negotiable: (1) *equity should never be an "add-on"; equity should be the foundation of everything we do.* The second equity non-negotiable is (2) *there is no opting out.* When it comes to doing equity work in education, we are all on the hook. Further, if we want to increase our chances of success in these endeavors, we should not try to go it alone, which is why the third equity non-negotiable is so important: (3) *we must build coalitions with other equity-minded people.*

Teachers as advocates for racial justice

Given my research on racism in education and the profes-sional development work I do with educators concerning these topics, it is not uncommon for white teachers or administrators to reach out to me with *what-would-you-do?* scenarios. Many times educators do this because they are looking for validation from me that they "handled" a racially charged situation in the "right way." But oftentimes they ask because they genuinely don't know if they did, and they want some suggestions for how they might do things differently next time.

While these are the most important types of questions I get to field, the reality is I don't have all the answers, and I certainly don't get it "right" all the time when it comes to racism and white privilege. In fact, the most impactful lessons I've learned over the years stem from all the times I've gotten it wrong. Also, I am acutely aware that my own positionality influences at all times how I am inclined to respond to these questions. I always begin by acknowledging these truths to the person who has presented the scenario to me, but nonetheless I try to offer some insights that might help them to create a more socially just learning environment for their students.

While the context varies from educator to educator, I find the scenario presented to me last year by Mr Bell, a white high-school teacher, to be quite formulaic. "I had a black male student in my class last year and his pants were so baggy that his rear end was practically hanging out," he began. "This had nothing to do with race – I just didn't want to look at his rear end! But as soon as I told him to pull up his pants, he told me I was racist! And I told him I was not being racist; I just didn't want to see his behind." It is at this point I am always expected to weigh in on the situation. In other words, I am expected to determine whether or not the teacher is indeed racist or (as the teacher inevitably hopes) the accusation of racism by the student of color is wrong. It is never lost on me how willing we are to allow a white person, who has never been present when any of these interactions occurred, completely to invalidate and undermine an account by a student of color of their own lived reality.

These conversations with white educators are not easy, but I've learned over the years that what often works in order to invite teachers and administrators to see the scenario from multiple standpoints is what I call the *both/ and* strategy. First, from Mr Bell's perspective, asking his black male student to pull up his pants had nothing to do with race and everything to do with "respect" or consideration for Mr Bell's authority and personal taste with regard to "proper" attire for students in the classroom. "Mr Bell, I'm going to take you at your word when you say you were not *intentionally* trying to be racist when you made that comment to your student," I began. "That said, let's interrogate your intentions for a moment."

This allowed me to bring into the conversation what the research tells us about how teachers disproportionately discipline the bodies of their students of color, especially with regard to dress (Morris 2005, 2007). It allowed me to probe Mr Bell's assumptions about dress, classroom etiquette, and the systems of inequality and privilege that underlie his assumptions. We then talked about the very plausible reasons why his student likely saw his directive – one of many behavioral directives the student was probably used to hearing, given what we know about the disparate experiences of white students and students of color in schools – as racist. This, of course, illuminated the important difference between *intention* and *impact* when it comes to racism: it might not have been Mr Bell's intention to reproduce the racial status quo, but, by immediately dismissing the student's claim of racism without further consideration and critical self-reflection, that is exactly what he did. He took a *colorblind* approach (e.g., "This has nothing to do with race!") as opposed to a *color-conscious* approach (e.g., "What are the ways in which white supremacy and beliefs about black racial inferiority, particularly my own implicit biases when it comes to black men and boys, might be showing up in this interaction?").

Much of the scholarship on inequalities in education, including my own, has looked to teachers as both the source and the potential solution to racial disparities in schooling (e.g., Lortie 1975; Noddings 1992; Allard 2004; Delpit 2006; Noguera 2008). While many of us continue to expect teachers to serve as social justice advocates in the classroom, the reality, with rare exception, is that this is not what teachers with whom I have worked over the years say inspired them to pursue careers in teaching. Still, despite the fact that most people do not go into teaching with the goal of working to dismantle institutional racism, they are on the hook for doing so, as we all are: recall that the second non-negotiable when it comes to equity work is *there is no opting out.*

How can teachers reject *colorblindness* and embrace *antiracism*? According to Pollock, there are four foundational principles for doing antiracism work in education: (1) rejecting false notions of human difference; (2) acknowledging lived experiences shaped along racial lines; (3) learning from diverse forms of knowledge and experience; and (4) challenging systems of racial inequality (2008: xx). Each of these principles comes with its own set of challenges for educators, but these challenges can be overcome.

First, it is important to acknowledge that teachers must be aware of and understand false notions of human difference before they can reject them. Remember, most of the teachers with whom I have worked still view race as a biological, genetic, or cultural phenomenon, not as a social, economic, and political construction. In other words, based on teachers' – especially white teachers' – limited knowledge of race and racism, they are more likely to perpetuate false notions of human difference than to challenge them.

The second principle of everyday antiracism, acknowledging lived experiences shaped along racial lines, is the opposite of being *colorblind*: it is about being *color-conscious*. It is acknowledging that race still matters and that our racial identities continue to impact our everyday experiences because we live in a racialized social system (Bonilla-Silva 1997). One challenge that comes with this principle is learning when that acknowledgement needs to be expressed and when it does not. This gets at Pollock's (2008) guiding question about knowing when identifying racial group differences helps and when it harms students of color.

Third, teachers must learn from diverse forms of knowledge and experience. This requires them actively to seek out sources that reflect a diverse array of racial perspectives. Ideally, these sources should be written by people of color, who are the only ones who can speak authoritatively about their everyday lived experiences in a society with an educational system that contributes to both the creation and the maintenance of the racial status quo. The challenge here is that it also requires white teachers to privilege the first-hand accounts of their students and colleagues of color, as opposed to immediately dismissing these accounts when they don't reflect their own experiences.

Fourth, antiracism doesn't start and stop in our class-rooms. As Pollock (2008) points out, doing everyday anti-racism means challenging *systems* of inequality. Unless we change structures – policies, practices, and laws – teachers' interventions for addressing racism in education are ulti-mately futile, since these types of strategies only work to alleviate the *consequences* of institutional racism and do so only at an individual level. Individual-level interven-tions alone cannot undo the racialized social structure (Bonilla-Silva 1997) which provides the context for the everyday interactions that occur in our classrooms. Indeed, colorblind classrooms are designed to legitimate the racial status quo, not to dismantle it. The challenge with this principle is the inevitable resistance that comes when we confront systems of power. As I often remind people, when you speak truth to power, power always speaks back.

How do teachers overcome these challenges in pursuit of color-consciousness and racial justice? The first three principles of everyday antiracism (Pollock 2008) are really about the education of teachers. The good news is that teachers don't have to be race scholars to engage in everyday antiracism; however, they do have to commit to ongoing personal and professional development, for their students and for themselves, and this is a lifelong endeavor. I consider professional development here to be any formal training facilitated by experts, whereas I think of personal development as the work in which educators engage on their own in order to advance their knowledge base and develop new skillsets.

I will discuss the responsibility administrators have when it comes to professional development in the next section, but here I want at least to state that professional development does not substitute for personal development: the two must go hand in hand. Also, I want to point out that our ultimate goal should be to embed knowledge about systems of inequality and privilege within our pre-K-12 curriculum and every teacher education program, so that teachers aren't having to learn basic information about race, gender, sexuality, etc., on the job. In other words, they should come to teaching with the foundational knowledge of race and racial inequality that is required for engaging in everyday antiracism.

In the interim, teachers are fortunate that, when it comes to personal development, we live in an era where access to critical, evidence-based information on race, white supremacy, white privilege, racism, etc., is easily accessible. As one example, Teaching Tolerance (www.tolerance.org) is a well-known repository of free social justice and anti-bias resources for educators who work with K-12 students. The Teaching Tolerance website includes lesson plans, webinars, toolkits, and readings for educators. This is just one of many online resources for those who want to engage in equity work.

Ideally, teachers should not engage in this work alone, however, as the third equity non-negotiable reminds us: *we must build coalitions with other equity-minded people*. I can't stress enough how critical it is that teachers who engage in antiracism work have a community of other social justice educators to support their personal and professional growth and well-being. This is especially the case for teachers whose principals are not strong leaders on equity issues – or, worse, openly antagonistic to their efforts.

My local school district offers a good example of community-building when it comes to equity work. Recently, one of our middle-school principals, in partnership with an elementary-school teacher at another school and one of our cultural liaisons who works with and supports black and African American students and their families, sent out a survey to all employees to gauge their interest in forming a coalition of educators committed to social justice work in education. Almost 20 percent of the teachers in our district indicated their desire to be part of this coalition. The original team members created an interactive website with resources for personal and professional growth. They also started book clubs with selections focused on social justice issues within and outside the realm of education. Currently, they are working on developing summer school options focused on advancing students' knowledge of social justice issues.

The personal and professional development this coalition offers is certainly valuable to the teachers who are taking part, but I think this group provides two other benefits that are just as important, if not more. First, by building a community of equity-minded educators, this coalition is serving as a social and professional safety net for teachers doing such work in the district, especially those who do not have supportive administrators and/or colleagues. Second, as the coalition grows and matures, these educators have the potential to change the climate in their schools, creating an environment where perspectives that undermine equity efforts are marginalized, not the other way around. In sum, these educators have the potential to change *systems* of inequality in their schools, achieving the fourth principle of everyday antiracism.

Finally, I used to feel frustrated when I would undertake professional development with teachers and someone would inevitably ask me if I could just give them a handout with clearly identified steps they could follow. I understand now that, more times than not, the request came not from a place of academic or professional laziness, or the belief that equity work is unimportant, but from a sense of agency: what can *I* do to address these inequalities? Unfortunately, there is no one list of steps that, if we follow it perfectly, will always achieve our desired results when it comes to racial justice in education. Indeed, there is no such thing as "perfection" when it comes to equity work. Nevertheless, I want to honor that sense of agency and provide teachers with some practical steps to help create a safe, welcoming, and inclusive learning environment for their students. This list is certainly not exhaustive, and it may require some modification depending on grade level, but it is an invitation to start rethinking some of our unexamined colorblind practices.

First, teachers must develop strategies that allow them to connect personally with students of color (and students from other historically marginalized groups as well). How do teachers know if students of color feel safe, welcome, and included in their classrooms, and, if they don't, what are some things teachers could do differently? They should be open to feedback, especially critical feedback, and convey this to their students. In addition, if students of color are willing to share their experiences, teachers should always strive for more listening and less talking. Equity work at its core is about relationship-building.

Second, teachers need to be extremely self-reflexive and critical about their classroom practices. They should not play "devil's advocate" in the classroom when it comes to racism. For example, teachers should not ask students to debate issues that include any standpoint that denies rights or affords basic humanity to people of color (or people from any historically marginalized group). Put simply, there are not two equally valid positions on racism; there is only one: it's unacceptable.

Further, teachers should not ask students of color to speak on behalf of their entire racial or ethnic group. For example, if a teacher has a Hmong American student in their class, they should not ask them to respond to questions or comments as if they are speaking for all people of Hmong descent (e.g., "Tell us, what do Hmong people think/feel about this?"). The racist implication here is that all people who identify as Hmong or Hmong American represent one homogeneous group, an assumption we would never imply when it comes to white people.

In the same vein, teachers should not ask students of color to educate them or their classmates on racial issues and experiences. Students of color attend school to *acquire* an education, not to serve as unpaid educators for their teachers and classmates. When we place this expectation on students of color, it represents yet another undue educational burden. We are always learning from our students, but white educators in particular should not ask, or expect, students of color to educate them on race, racism, and/or white supremacy; we must educate ourselves and then educate others in our sphere of influence, including our colleagues and students.

Third, teachers should always be examining the curriculum they use through a critical multicultural lens. Is the curriculum racially inclusive? Is it culturally relevant? Does it perpetuate stereotypes and false notions of human difference? How many readings are students assigned that are written by people of color? Today, teachers are overwhelmingly required to rely on a standardized curriculum, but, whenever and wherever they have the autonomy to supplement that curriculum, they should be choosing materials that reflect a range of racial and ethnic experiences (as well as the experiences of people of other historically marginalized groups). Further, if the curriculum they are required to use is Euro- or white-centric (and most curriculums are), teachers should acknowledge it, problematize it, and work to change it.

Administrators as advocates for racial justice

Administrators should be outspoken, committed, steadfast leaders for achieving racial equity in their districts. However, bear in mind that most administrators are former teachers, and, as we have already established, teachers generally support the notion of *equity* but tend to hold problematic views when it comes to race and racism. While I believe administrators *should* be the prophetic voice on racial justice in their districts, I am acutely aware that most administrators, especially white administrators, like the teachers and staff they lead, are not experts on these issues. Of the administrators with whom I have worked – most of whom are white, straight, cisgender men (especially at the upper levels of administration) – very few have had any formal training on identifying and addressing social inequalities in education. Nonetheless, they, too, are on the hook, as the second equity non-negotiable reminds us.

Administrators, just like teachers, must be committed to personal and professional growth on issues of racial justice. In the previous section, I focused on personal development. Here, I want to focus on professional development because it is administrators that bear the responsibility of ensuring their teachers and staff (as well as themselves) have access to critical, evidence-based professional development when it comes to equity. Further, professional development on race and racism in education cannot be a one-time deal. Just as personal development is a lifelong endeavor, professional development should be an ongoing commitment in every district.

In my experience, unfortunately, the first place administrators look for professional development opportunities, consultation, and equity assessments for their schools or their district is outside their own communities, and they are often willing to spend several thousand dollars for these services. During the year I was conducting research in the Lakeview Public School District, a public discussion took place between the superintendent and school board about whether tens of thousands of dollars should be spent on bringing in an educational consulting firm from California to study equity issues in their district. If the superintendent and school board had simply contacted their own institutional research office, they would have found that I and perhaps others who were also well acquainted with the schools were already conducting such research. Also, recall the assembly I attended at Lyons High that illuminated the importance of including bullying in my research study. The district flew in an educational consultant from across the country to speak about the importance of celebrating difference and practicing tolerance in their school and community.

The point I want to make here is not that administrators should look *only* in their own backyards for direction when it comes to equity work, but they should start there. People who do equity work that live in the same community are invested in creating and maintaining a school system where students can thrive. If they have children themselves, they will likely attend those schools, and, even if they don't have school-aged children, as community members they still have a vested interest in a strong, local public school system. Further, people who live in the community that do equity work understand the dynamics of the community and school district and will likely continue to reside in the area even after their work with the district is finished. Outside educational consultants do not have first-hand knowledge of the school district or share the same level of investment in the community.

Where should administrators look to find such people? First, they should start in house. This may seem intuitive, but I know of accounts where people of color were essentially hired to do equity work in their district and then perpetually overlooked when it came to orchestrating and leading professional development on these issues. Second, if there are any institutions of higher learning in the community, administrators should investigate whether there are faculty members who engage in social justice work, particularly if that work focuses on equity in pre-K-12 schools. Third, administrators should identify any social justice or diversity-oriented organizations in the community. Many of these types of organizations offer professional development or consulting services.

The importance of starting in our own backyard when looking for professional development opportunities, equity assessments, or other types of consulting work is that it goes right to the heart of community-building. If administrators are serious about dismantling institutional racism in their schools and communities, they should cultivate relationships with other local organizations that will support such endeavors. However, while buy-in from community partners can be extremely helpful, lack of buy-in is no excuse to derail critical equity work in a school district. Sometimes school districts will have to model the importance of this work for their community.

Superintendents and other administrators should not only prioritize equity work in their districts, but incentivize it. There are several ways to do this. Teachers can be awarded grants to implement interventions designed to address inequities, including racism, in their classrooms. Teachers and staff who undergo advanced training on equity issues can serve as equity consultants in their schools. Teachers who earn graduate credits in social justice-related studies can move up on the salary schedule. These are just a few suggestions, and while some may believe this is simply rewarding people for work they should be doing anyway, I disagree. Yes, it's true that we should all be engaging in this work regardless, but I believe incentivizing it demonstrates the importance a school district places on antiracism efforts specifically and social justice work in general.

Finally, just as I provided some practical suggestions for teachers in the last section, I want to do the same for administrators based on my experiences working with superintendents and other school district leaders on these issues. The information that follows is meant to serve only as a conversation starter, but, to be clear, these conversations need to happen for us to begin the transformational work required to dismantle institutional racism in our schools.

Administrators, particularly superintendents, recognize that people in their schools and in their communities are looking to them for their leadership on these issues. They know the stakes are high and that concerns related to race, gender, sexuality, ability status, etc., are sensitive for many, if not most, of their stakeholders. Given these are not areas of expertise for most administrators, the thought of engaging in antiracism work can lead to a heightened sense of anxiety about potential missteps and fear of an impending (white) backlash from teachers, families, community members, and even other administrators.

In my experience, administrators, particularly white, male-identifying administrators, often think they should not show any vulnerability or weakness in their roles as district leaders, and, unfortunately, this simply doesn't work, especially when it comes to challenging systems of inequality and privilege. When administrators attempt to lead on these issues based on an ideology that anything less than perfection is unacceptable, they are setting themselves, as well as their staff and students, up for failure. As we have already established, there is no "always getting it right" when we engage in social justice work. White administrators in particular need to model for their white teachers, staff, and students what it looks like to make a misstep, learn from it, make amends, and start again with a commitment to do better next time. With humility and integrity, they should acknowledge the significance of their own social location when it comes to engaging in this work and admit they don't know it all when it comes to race and racism. But at the same time they should convey their commitment to educating themselves and advancing racial equity in their districts.

Like teachers, administrators must always be extremely self-reflexive and willing to ask themselves and their colleagues the hard questions. For example, if a white superintendent says they are committed to racial justice, but every member of their leadership team is white, this should give them pause. Further, the same questions I posed to teachers above apply to district leadership, too: how do administrators know their teachers and staff of color feel safe, welcome, and included in their district, and, if they don't, what could administrators do differently? Administrators must be willing to learn from their employees of color, privileging their first-hand accounts of what it is like to work in their schools, districts, and communities, particularly in locales that are predominantly white. Again, more listening and less talking is the goal.

Finally, administrators should not go it alone either. In this section, I've mentioned the importance of forming community partnerships when it comes to professional development; however, administrators also need to be in community with others who are committed to personal development on these issues. If administrators aren't experts on social justice – and most aren't – they can and should reach out to people who are, starting in their own backyard with people who are committed to and invested in achieving equity in their local school system. Finally, as we will see in the next section, superintendents, in particular, need the support of their local school boards when doing equity work.

School board members as advocates for racial justice

I have yet to meet a person who could name every member of their local school board. In fact, I rarely meet a person who can name one. Even when it comes to teachers, most cannot name more than one or two members of their local school board – if that – and these are the elected officials who are making decisions that impact their livelihoods. This should give all of us pause, especially if we care about equity and social justice work in education.

Given the nature of the work I do, I envisioned running for my local school board at some point in the future; I did not plan to run for office in the spring of 2017. However, after the outcome of the 2016 presidential election, I felt I could not put it off any longer. Clearly, I was not alone, given the number of Americans, including a record number of women, who ran for public office on a progressive social agenda following Donald Trump's election. When I threw my hat in the ring, I knew nothing about running a campaign. Fortunately, I was mentored by others in my community who had the relevant experience.

In my local school district, the board of education is comprised of nine members, including myself, who serve three-year rotating terms. Each spring, people who live within the school district boundaries have the opportunity to vote for three candidates. The year I ran, one incumbent decided to step down, leaving one open seat. Four of us, two incumbents and two newcomers, competed for the three available spots. However, in many local races, particularly in smaller communities, it is not uncommon for candidates to run uncontested. This should be concerning to all of us who support a strong democratic process for electing candidates to public office. It should also concern us that more people are typically interested in national elections as opposed to state and, especially, local elections. In reality, it is the people who are elected to office in our own communities who often have the most power to make the kinds of decisions that impact our everyday lives.

The information I learned when running for office was both invaluable and at times troubling – and I had to learn all of it in a very short amount of time. One of the early lessons I learned was that you have to spend money even when running for local office; campaign materials are not free. I was also dismayed by the other obstacles in our election processes that prevent good candidates, particularly candidates from historically marginalized groups, from running.

I share this information about my experience to highlight several key points when it comes to school boards and social justice work in education. First, according to data collected in 2002 by Frederick Hess at the University of Virginia for the National School Boards Association (NSBA), school boards tend to be overwhelmingly white, especially in more rural areas or districts with smaller boards (four in five small district boards are at least 90 percent white). Second, while school board elections in the US remain overwhelmingly non-partisan races, those who run for seats on their local school boards are not non-partisan. According to the NSBA study, "Respondents generally report their political views as being moderate or conservative, with fewer than one in five labeling themselves liberal. Even in large districts, which are generally regarded as liberal strongholds, a majority of respondents identify themselves as moderate and more respondents term themselves conservative than liberal" (Hess 2002: 5). Third, in terms of gender composition, local school boards tend to have greater representation by women than we find at the state and national level, but men still outnumber women (to my knowledge, there is no current data on transgender school board members). Fourth, relatively few school board members have a background in education; most come from business and professional backgrounds. Finally, the NSBA data shows that incumbents are rarely unseated in school board races.

In sum, this data sheds a light on the types of people who typically make decisions about how their school districts operate. While there are a number of actions school boards can take to advance racial justice, they must be willing to exert the political will to do so, and this depends on who is sitting around the table when such discussions take place. The bottom line is that the outcome of school board elections matter when it comes to equity work.

Representation also matters. If students of color make up 30 percent of the population in a school district, and a school board has no members of color, this should be of concern in a district that claims it supports racial equity. The guiding question for me is always "Does this school board reflect the student body that it serves?" In my own community, I work with others to identify and support strong candidates that will increase diversity on the board in a number of ways and will be ardent supporters of social justice work.

In addition, if school boards want to advance racial justice, they need valid, reliable data (1) to identify any equity gaps in their districts and (2) to assess if those gaps are being addressed. School board members typically view a lot of statistical reports during meetings. When I was elected, I immediately noticed a few empirical shortcomings in some of our reports. The two biggest concerns for me were (1) that data was not always disaggregated by subgroups (e.g., how can we know if students of color are disproportionately suspended if the data on school discipline is not broken down by race and ethnicity?);

and (2) that there were flaws in certain survey measures, such as the use of double-barreled questions and/or the use of non-inclusive categories, especially with regard to gender identity/gender expression. Now, to be fair, these were issues I immediately noticed because I am a researcher and do this kind of work for a living, but, again, it highlights the importance of whom we elect to our school boards.

Once we were able to address these methodological shortcomings, we gained a much more nuanced under-standing of where we stood in terms of equity gaps, which also meant the district could develop better interventions for addressing them. School boards and school district personnel should never utilize survey instruments devel-oped in house that have not been vetted by one or more persons who have expertise in survey design. This might be done by a district's institutional research specialist or in consultation with faculty in higher education or industry professionals.

Further, when we find equity gaps that exist in our districts – and we will – we shouldn't try to shove these findings under the rug or attempt to explain them away. Rather, we should acknowledge them, problematize them, and commit to addressing them. In this same vein, school board members, just like administrators and teachers, must be open to critical feedback and change. *This is the way we've always done it* or *that's not our job* is a dangerous attitude, especially when it comes to engaging in equity work.

Finally, I think it's important to point out that, while school boards may develop or support policies that encourage and/or require administrators, teachers, and staff to engage in equity training, school board members can generally avoid having to undergo any personal or professional development themselves on issues related to racism, sexism, ableism, transphobia, homophobia, etc. This is unacceptable. There is no excuse for school board members to use racially insensitive language or advance outdated racial stereotypes, whether they are sitting at the board table or are out in the community. If school boards want to dismantle systems of privilege and oppression in their districts, every board member needs to be held personally accountable for putting in the hard work that is required. Doing otherwise demonstrates a lack of commitment to antiracism and equity work in their district.

Community members as advocates for racial justice

The last group I want to address as potential advocates for racial justice is community members. Originally, I thought of directing my final suggestions to families of students specifically – after all, they share a direct connection to their local schools via their children. However, I opted to expand this discussion to community members for two reasons: (1) families *are* community members, and thus it is implied going forward that I am speaking to them in addition to non-school families; and (2), as previously mentioned, whether or not a community member has children or their children have already matriculated through the school system, we all have a vested interest in the success of our local public schools.

When it comes to advancing racial justice in a school district, one of the most important things community members can do, as discussed in the previous section, is vote. They should vote for school board candidates who are committed to addressing equity gaps in their schools and have fundamental knowledge about how systems of inequality and privilege work. Community members should ask candidates (1) where they stand on issues related to race and social justice; (2) to detail previous work they have done to address racial inequalities; and (3) to outline an agenda for how they would address equity gaps in their district if elected. If candidates don't have good answers to these questions, or attempt to deflect them, community members should take the lack of responses or *non-responses* as their answer and vote accordingly.

Further, community members are important stakeholders in their local public school system. They have every right to hold their school district accountable for advancing equity in general and racial justice specifically, and they should. Just as it is important for teachers to form coalitions to support one another, coalitions are important for community members committed to social justice in education. These may be formal or informal groups. Community groups may take on special projects in order to support the school district in their antiracism efforts. For example, one such group in my community, Kids First, Equity Now, collected money last year to buy books for students of all ages that centered the experiences of people of color and featured racial justice themes. They gave these books to students of color in the district free of charge. Community groups can also sponsor events that raise awareness of equity issues in schools and facilitate public discussions about how to close equity gaps.

Finally, community groups that want to advance antiracism in their local school system should serve as advocates for students of color and their families. When racially charged incidents occur in their local schools, they should support students of color and their families in the fight for racial justice. To that end, community members should hold educators accountable, especially the school board and superintendent, when racial disparities go unaddressed.

Moving forward

Because racism is so ubiquitous in the United States, many people are discouraged that nothing can ever be done to change things, but this is not true. First, social systems by their very nature are dynamic. In *Paradoxes of Gender*, Judith Lorber (1994) reminded us that gender as an institution had changed in the past and would continue to do so in the future, but that change did not necessitate gender equality. As Lorber argued, for that to happen, gender must first be made visible.

Race is a social construction; it can be deconstructed. But to do so it must be made visible, and this is why colorblindness will never end racism. As we have seen in this book, colorblindness for teachers rarely manifests as an outright denial that they "see race" – although that does happen. Rather, colorblindness operates in a *now-you-see-race-now-you-don't* fashion, almost like a moving target that is hard to pin down, and, if we can't pin it down, we can't address it.

In this book, I have illustrated a number of discursive strategies teachers use to advance colorblind racism (Bonilla-Silva 2003). Sometimes they rely on abstract liberalism and claim "reverse discrimination" to deny supporting race-based policies that might be able to close equity gaps. Sometimes they argue that the "real" culprit when it comes to racism is the problematic "culture" of people of color, and sometimes they argue that the culprit is something other than race, such as social class. In my experience, teachers do this not out of maliciousness but out of ignorance and, at times, even a sense of benevolence (Esposito and Romano 2014). Yet, when it comes to addressing racism in schools, I am concerned less with the *intentions* of their actions and more with the *impact* of their actions, especially the impact on students of color.

As we have seen in this chapter, there is a way forward. We begin with our equity non-negotiables: (1) *equity is not an add-on; it is the foundation of everything we do*; (2) *there is no opting out when it comes to equity work*; and (3) *we must build coalitions of equity-minded people*. Beyond these non-negotiables, I have provided some suggestions for engaging in antiracism for people coming to this work from multiple entry points, such as teachers, administrators, school boards, and community members. These suggestions are by no means exhaustive; if anything, they are meant to serve as catalysts for what should be a lifelong commitment to dismantling systems of racial inequality in education.

Postscript: Social justice canaries in the coalmine

I want to close this book on a personal note that I hope further solidifies why we need urgently to address color-blind racism in schools. In the second chapter of this book, I introduced readers to Ms Coxey at Lyons High as one of the most social justice-oriented teachers I had ever known. The second is Ms Green, an elementary-school teacher in Wisconsin. I met Ms Green two years ago, and we immediately bonded over our passion for social justice work in education. What struck me about Ms Green, other than the fact she is a ball of energy, was her commitment to creating a safe, welcome, and inclusive classroom for all her students, and she didn't just talk the talk: in addition to all the responsibilities she had on her plate as a teacher, she made time for both personal and professional development related to racism, ableism, transphobia, etc. In sum, if someone asked me to provide examples of model teachers who are strong social justice advocates in their classrooms and in their schools, it would be Ms Coxey and Ms Green.

By the time I was wrapping up this book, both teachers were on medical leave because the stress associated with the persistent and ongoing attempts to undermine their equity work with students had taken a toll on their health.

Shortly after my research at Lyons High ended, Ms Coxey, after years of pushback from administrators and colleagues over her social justice efforts, left her teaching position there to go to work for an alternative school in the same district that branded itself a "compassion school," where trauma-informed pedagogy was valued over more punitive approaches. She wrote to me of her early experiences there:

> Within days, the police began arriving to arrest children for minor infractions. In late September, four police arrested a female student who was working on math in my classroom for a minor charge, which she wasn't guilty of. That arrest was followed by two more arrests the next week, and two marginalized children who were traumatized by the arrests threatened to kill themselves while in my classroom. The principal was trying to pull children from my classroom morning circle, and I refused to send them out of the sanctuary of circle. He came into my classroom during circle and pulled a student out anyway. After years of seeing and hearing about so much violence against children, I was diagnosed with PTSD. I left my classroom on medical leave in

October and won't be returning to teaching until I am healed. I returned to the school last week to pack up my belongings. Ninety-eight percent of my room was as I left it. However, what they took down was telling: graduation photos (many of which were students of color), a Minnesota Humanities Bill of Rights display, a Teaching Tolerance "All (religions, ethnicities, sexual orientations) are Welcome Here" poster, a poster of a young man of color who is dressed in street clothes but sees himself in the mirror as a doctor with an inspirational poem, and an African portrait done by a student. Apparently the district has "lost" the Bill of Rights display, but they are looking for it ....

Ms Green didn't have police coming into her classroom on a regular basis, but her efforts to create a socially just learning environment for her students were also continually thwarted by her principal because these efforts clashed with the latter's conservative political and religious beliefs. Each time Ms Green would persist in her equity work, and each time her principal would persist in undermining it. Nevertheless, Ms Green stuck it out until her health began to suffer, and then, like Ms Coxey, she felt she had no choice but to take a medical leave until she was healthy enough to return to the classroom. When I spoke with her recently, she told me through tears, "Laurie, I just want to be in my classroom right now. I just want to be with my kids. But I am so depleted and discouraged, I feel like I have nothing left to give."

I view what happened to Ms Coxey and Ms Green as cautionary tales; they are the social justice canaries in the coalmine. Imagine the impact these two teachers could have on equity in their schools and in their districts if they were given the support they needed by their administrators to do so. Now imagine the students, especially the students of color and students from other historically marginalized groups, who no longer have these two advocates in their classrooms and in their schools.

In my research on social inequalities in education, I always acknowledge that we have a responsibility to hold individual teachers accountable whenever they perpetuate prejudice or discrimination, but we cannot lay the blame for institutional racism solely at the feet of teachers, especially when we don't give them the resources and the support they need to work to dismantle it. If we are going to hold teachers accountable, we must hold the administrators who stand in the way of racial justice accountable. Put simply, we cannot expect teachers to serve as social justice advocates in our schools but then undermine them at every turn. When teachers such as Ms Coxey and Ms Green step away from education, we all lose, but students of color lose the most.

Alexander, M. (2010) *The New Jim Crow: Mass Incarceration in the Age of Colorblindness*. New York: New Press.

Allard, A. C. (2004) "Speaking of gender: teachers' metaphorical constructs of male and female students," *Gender and Education* 16: 347–63.

Baggett, H. C., and C. G. Simmons (2017) "A case study of white teacher candidates' conceptions of racial profiling in educational contexts," *Journal of Education* 197(1): 41–51.

Barshay, J. (2018) "Early evidence of a 'Trump effect' on bullying in schools," *The Hechinger Report*, September 17.

Blau, J. R. (2003) *Race in the Schools: Perpetuating White Dominance?* Boulder, CO: Lynn Rienner.

Bobo, L. D. (1999) "Prejudice as group position: microfoundations of a sociological approach to racism and race relations," *Journal of Social Issues* 55: 445–72.

Bonilla-Silva, E. (1997) "Rethinking racism: toward a structural interpretation," *American Sociological Review* 62: 465–80.

Bonilla-Silva, E. (2001) *White Supremacy and Racism in the Post-Civil Rights Era*. Boulder, CO: Lynn Rienner.

Bonilla-Silva, E. (2003) *Racism without Racists: Color-Blind Racism and the Persistence of Racial Inequality in the United States*. Lanham, MD: Rowman & Littlefield.

Bonilla-Silva, E. (2006) *Racism without Racists: Color-Blind Racism and the Persistence of Racial Inequality in the United States*. 2nd edn, Lanham, MD: Rowman & Littlefield.

References

Bonilla-Silva, E. (2018) *Racism without Racists: Color-Blind Racism and the Persistence of Racial Inequality in the United States.* 5th edn, Lanham, MD: Rowman & Littlefield.

Bonilla-Silva, E., and D. G. Embrick (2008) "Black, honorary white, white: the future of race in the United States?," pp. 33–48 in *Mixed Messages: Multiracial Identities in the Color-Blind Era*, ed. D. L. Brunsma. Boulder, CO: Lynne Rienner.

Burke, Meghan (2018) *Colorblind Racism.* Cambridge: Polity.

Byrd, C. M. (2015) "The associations of intergroup interactions and school racial socialization with academic motivation," *Journal of Educational Research* 108(1): 10–21.

Call-Cummings, M., and S. Martinez (2017) "'It wasn't racism; it was more misunderstanding': white teachers, latino/a students, and racial battle fatigue," *Race Ethnicity and Education* 20(4): 561–74.

Chapman, T. K. (2013) "You can't erase race! Using CRT to explain the presence of race and racism in majority white suburban schools," *Studies in the Cultural Politics of Education* 34(4): 611–27.

Cobb, J. S. (2017) "Inequality frames: how teachers inhabit color-blind ideology," *Sociology of Education* 90(4): 315–32.

Coleman, J. S., and T. Hoffer (1987) *Public and Private High Schools: The Impact of Communities.* New York: Basic Books.

Collins, P. H. (2000) *Black Feminist Thought: Knowledge, Consciousness, and the Politics of Empowerment.* 2nd edn, New York: Routledge.

Delpit, L. (2006) *Other People's Children: Cultural Conflict in the Classroom.* 2nd edn, New York: New Press.

Demoiny, S. B. (2017) "Are you ready? Elementary pre-service teachers' perceptions about discussing race in social studies," *Multicultural Education* 24(2): 25–33.

DePouw, C. (2012) "When culture implies deficit: placing race at the center of Hmong American education," *Race Ethnicity and Education* 15(2): 223–39.

References

Doane, A. W. (2017) "Beyond color-blindness: (re)theorizing racial ideology," *Sociological Perspectives* 60(5): 975–91.

Dovidio, J. F., and S. L. Gaertner (2000) "Aversive racism and selection decisions: 1989 and 1999," *Psychological Science* 11: 319–23.

Dovidio, J. F., S. Gaertner and T. Saguy (2015) "Color-blindness and commonality: included but invisible?" *American Behavioral Scientist* 59(11): 1518–38.

Downey, D. B., and S. Pribesh (2004) "When race matters: teachers' evaluations of students' classroom behavior," *Sociology of Education* 77: 267–82.

Duncan, G. A. (2005) "Critical race ethnography in education: narrative, inequality and the problem of epistemology," *Race Ethnicity and Education* 8: 93–114.

Esposito, L., and V. Romano (2014) "Upholding racial inequality in the name of black Empowerment," *Western Journal of Black Studies* 38(2): 69–83.

Esposito, L., and V. Romano (2016) "Benevolent racism and the co-optation of the Black Lives Matter movement," *Western Journal of Black Studies* 40(3): 161–73.

Everitt, J. G. (2013) "Inhabitants moving in: prospective sense-making and the reproduction of inhabited institutions in teacher education," *Symbolic Interactions* 36(2): 177–96.

Farago, F., K. Sanders, and L. Gaias (2015) "Addressing race and racism in early childhood: challenges and opportunities," *Advances in Early Education & Day Care* 19: 29–66.

Farkas, G. (1996) *Human Capital or Cultural Capital? Ethnicity and Poverty Groups in an Urban School District*. New York: Aldine Transaction.

Ferguson, A. A. (2001) *Bad Boys: Public Schools in the Making of Black Masculinity*. Ann Arbor: University of Michigan Press.

Ferguson, R. F. (1998) "Teachers' perceptions and expectations and the black–white test score gap," pp. 460–507 in *The Black–White*

Test Score Gap, ed. C. Jenks and M. Phillips. Washington, DC: Brookings Institution Press.

Fernández, L. (2002) "Telling stories about school: using critical race and Latino critical theories to document Latina/Latino education and resistance," *Qualitative Inquiry* 8: 45–65.

Forman, T. A. (2004) "Color-blind racism and racial indifference: the role of racial apathy in facilitating enduring inequalities," pp. 67–119 in *The Changing Terrain of Race and Ethnicity*, ed. M. Krysan and A. E. Lewis. New York: Russell Sage Foundation.

Foster, M. (1990) "The politics of race: through the eyes of African-American teachers," *Journal of Education* 172: 123–41.

Gershenson, S., S. B. Holt, and N. Papageorge (2016) "Who believes in me? The effect of student–teacher demographic match on teacher expectations," *Economics of Education Review* 52: 209–24.

Gregory, A., and E. Fergus (2017) "Social and emotional learning and equity in school discipline," *Future of Children* 27(1): 117–36.

Harry, B., and J. Klingner (2006) *Why Are So Many Minority Students in Special Education? Understanding Race & Disability in Schools.* New York: Teachers College Press.

Hartmann, D., P. R. Croll, R. Larson, J. Gerteis, and A. Manning (2017) "Colorblindness as identity: key determinants, relations to ideology, and implications for attitudes about race and policy," *Sociological Perspectives* 60(5): 866–88.

Henfield, M. S. (2011) "Black male adolescents navigating microaggressions in a traditionally white middle school: a qualitative study," *Multicultural Counseling and Development* 39(3): 141–55.

Hess, F. M. (2002) *School Boards at the Dawn of the 21st Century: Conditions and Challenges of District Governance*, National Schools Board Administration official report, www.nvasb.org/assets/school_boards_at_the_dawn_of_the_21st_century.pdf.

Joseph, N. M., K. M. Viesca, and M. Bianco (2016) "Black female adolescents and racism in schools: experiences in a colorblind society," *High School Journal* 100(1): 4–25.

Kozol, J. (2005) *The Shame of the Nation: The Restoration of Apartheid Schooling in America*. New York: Three Rivers Press.

Lewis, A. E. (2004) "What group? Studying whites and whiteness in the era of color-blindness," *Sociological Theory* 22: 623–46.

Lewis, A. E. (2005) *Race in the Schoolyard: Negotiating the Color Line in Classrooms and Communities*. New Brunswick, NJ: Rutgers University Press.

Lipsitz, G. (2006) *The Possessive Investment in Whiteness: How White People Profit from Identity Politics*. Philadelphia: Temple University Press.

López, G. R., and V. A. Vázquez (2006) "They don't speak English": interrogating (racist) ideologies and perceptions of school personnel in a Midwestern state," *International Electronic Journal for Leadership in Learning* 10(29), http://iejll.journalhosting.ucalgary.ca/iejll/index.php/ijll/article/view/629/291.

Lorber, J. (1994) *Paradoxes of Gender*. New Haven, CT: Yale University Press.

Lortie, D. C. (1975) *Schoolteacher: A Sociological Study*. Chicago: University of Chicago Press.

McDermott, M. (2015) "Color-blind and color-visible identity among American whites," *American Behavioral Scientist* 59(11): 1452–73.

Modica, M. (2015) "Unpacking the 'colorblind approach': accusations of racism at a friendly, mixed-race school," *Race, Ethnicity and Education* 18(3): 396–418.

Morris, E. W. (2005) " 'Tuck in that shirt!' Race, class, gender, and discipline in an urban school," *Sociological Perspectives* 48: 25–48.

Morris, E. W. (2007) " 'Ladies' or 'loudies'? Perceptions and experiences of black girls in classrooms," *Youth & Society* 38(4): 490–515.

References

National Center for Education Statistics (2017) https://nces.ed.gov.

Noddings, N. (1992) *The Challenge to Care in Schools: An Alternative Approach to Education*. New York: Teachers College Press.

Noguera, P. A. (2008) *The Trouble with Black Boys … and Other Reflections on Race, Equity, and the Future of Public Education*. San Francisco: Jossey-Bass.

Parsons, A. A., K. M. Walsemann, S. J. Jones, H. Knopf, and C. E. blake (2018) "Parental involvement: rhetoric of inclusion in an environment of exclusion," *Journal of Contemporary Ethnography* 47(1): 113–39.

Perkins, H. W., D. W. Craig, and J. M. Perkins (2011) "Using social norms to reduce bullying: a research intervention among adolescents in five middle schools," *Group Processes & Intergroup Relations* 14(5): 703–22.

Pettigrew, T., and Meertens, R. (1995) "Subtle and blatant prejudice in Western Europe," *European Journal of Social Psychology*, 25: 57–75.

Pollock, M. (2008) *Everyday Antiracism: Getting Real about Race in School*. New York: New Press.

Priest, N., R. Perry, A. Ferdinand, Y. Paradies, and M. Kelaher (2014) "Experiences of racism, racial/ethnic attitudes, motivated fairness and mental health outcomes among primary and secondary school students," *Journal of Youth and Adolescence* 43(10): 1672–87.

Rong, X. L. (1996) "Effects of race and gender on teachers' perception of the social behavior of elementary students," *Urban Education* 31: 261–90.

Schofield, J. (2009) "The colorblind perspective in school: causes and consequences," pp. 259–84 in *Multicultural Education: Issues and Perspectives*, ed. J. A. Banks and C. A. McGee Banks. New York: John Wiley.

Scott, K. A. (2003) "In girls, out girls, and always black: African-American girls' friendships," *Sociological Studies of Children and Youth* 9: 179–207.

References

Sears, D. O., and P. J. Henry (2003) "The origins of symbolic racism," *Journal of Personality and Social Psychology* 85: 259–75.

Southern Poverty Law Center (2016) *After Election Day: The Trump Effect: The Impact of the 2016 Presidential Election on Our Nation's Schools*, www.splcenter.org/sites/default/files/the_trump_effect.pdf.

Stoll, L. C. (2013) *Race and Gender in the Classroom: Teachers, Privilege, and Enduring Social Inequalities*. Lanham, MD: Lexington Books.

Stoll, L. C., and M. Klein (2018) "Not in my backyard: how abstract liberalism and colorblind diversity undermines racial justice," pp. 217–40 in *Challenging the Status Quo: Diversity, Democracy, and Equality in the 21st Century*, ed. S. Collins and D. Embrick. Leiden: Brill.

University of California Regents v. *Bakke*, 438 US 265 – Supreme Court 1978, http://cdn.ca9.uscourts.gov/datastore/general/2017/11/21/University%20of%20California%20Regents%20v.%20Bakke,%20438%20US%20265%20-%20Supreme%20Court%201978%20-.pdf.

Valenzuela, A. (1999) *Subtractive Schooling: U.S.-Mexican Youth and the Politics of Caring*. Albany: State University of New York Press.

Vittrup, B. (2016) "Early childhood teachers' approaches to multicultural education and perceived barriers to disseminating anti-bias messages," *Multicultural Education* 23: 37–41.

Wetherell, M., and J. Potter (1992) *Mapping the Language of Racism*. London: Sage.

Wilson, W. J. (1978) *The Declining Significance of Race: Blacks and Changing American Institutions*. Chicago: University of Chicago Press.

Wood, D., R. Kaplan, and V. C. McLoyd (2007) "Gender differences in the educational expectations of urban, low-income African American youth: The role of parents and the school," *Journal of Youth and Adolescence* 36: 417–27.

Index

Index

Index